FLOOD STAGE

Opening The Windows Of Heaven

by Oral Roberts

"Prove me now – saith the Lord – I will open the windows of heaven and pour you out a blessing where there is not room enough to contain it" – not a trickle, not a stream, not a river, but A FLOOD!

Unless otherwise indicated,
all Scripture quotations are from
the King James Version of the Bible.

CONTENTS

READ THIS BOOK IN 7 DAYS OR LESS . . .

WHAT IS FLOOD STAGE?

God's plan from the beginning has been for us to live our lives in the FLOOD STAGE of His continuous blessing: spiritually, physically, financially. So before we go any further, I want to explain what I mean by FLOOD STAGE, because you will be coming across these words all through this book.

You, no doubt, know about a flood stage in the natural. It is when the rains come and keep coming. Every gully, every stream, every river, and every lake is filled — and the rains keep coming. And when there is no longer any place for the rain to go, the land is at flood stage. This is in the natural.

But in this book I want to tell you about the good kind of FLOOD STAGE. A *supernatural* FLOOD STAGE that will soak your life with God's blessings until you are no longer merely "existing" spiritually, physically, or financially. You come out of the emptiness, the dryness, the helplessness, AND the hopelessness into God's FLOOD STAGE of good things.

God has a system He works through. He created that system. He tells us to get involved with Him in a way that we will prove Him to ourselves as our . . .

> SOURCE SYSTEM,
> PROSPERITY SYSTEM,
> HEALTH SYSTEM.

God says, "Prove me now herewith, saith the Lord, if I will not open the windows of heaven, and pour you out a blessing where there is not room enough to contain it" (Malachi 3:10). When there is not room enough to contain it — like the rain that keeps soaking the land until it overflows and has to go somewhere — that is when you get into FLOOD STAGE

READ THIS BOOK IN 7 DAYS OR LESS . . .

living. God's blessings fill your life until your whole being is soaked, and yet the blessings keep coming. You are in FLOOD STAGE to the extent that God BLESSES you and MAKES you a BLESSING. This is what every true believer wants above all — to be *blessed* of God so much that He *makes* you a *bless-ing* to many, many others.

Living a casual Christian life means we are too often in the trickle stage . . . or the stream stage . . . but seldom in the river stage . . . and almost never in the FLOOD STAGE. The blessings we receive are too few and too small. Whereas when we start releasing our faith — turning it loose to God — we "prove God" as He has told us to. He will give us PROOF of himself by blessing us spiritually, physically, and financially — then put us in position to BE A BLESSING, ABUNDANTLY.

These are not just words I am saying about FLOOD STAGE. They are real, they are life!

God himself tells you and me in His own Holy Word to prove Him. We *can* prove Him. He *is* provable. But He says it is up to us to meet the conditions of the way His system works. He says, "I am God, I change not" (Malachi 3:6). Therefore we must do the changing; otherwise, we beat our heads up against His system. God is a good God and when we work with Him and His system, we allow Him to open the flood gates of heaven in our lives. Then we will personally know WHO GOD IS . . . and experience FLOOD STAGE living.

That is what this book is all about.

Oral Roberts

READ THIS BOOK IN 7 DAYS OR LESS . . .

(left to right) Oral, Richard, Lindsay, and Evelyn Roberts

The Roberts family is a candidate for FLOOD STAGE. GIVING/LIVING is the biblical way Evelyn and I, our son Richard, and daughter-in-law Lindsay continue to "prove God" to *bless* us and make us a *blessing*. We, like so many, know the blessings of God in the trickle stage . . . the stream stage. We even know the river stage at times. But those times we come into FLOOD STAGE are the greatest of all. We have set our faith on a straight line to God to know Him in FLOOD STAGE blessings!

CHAPTER ONE

YOU AND JESUS TALKING

*Beloved, I wish above all things that thou mayest
prosper and be in health, even as thy soul
prospereth.* —III John 2

WHAT IF YOU and the Lord Jesus were talking and He told you
your faith could rise to FLOOD STAGE? What if He told you
your faith could go from a trickle, from a stream, from a river
all the way to FLOOD STAGE?

What if He showed you how He could take your weakness
and turn it into strength . . . your sickness into health . . .
your wrong relationship with God into a right relationship for
your peace and forgiveness . . . and your financial need into
becoming a FLOOD of financial blessings?

Well, on the basis of all Jesus has said in the Holy Word of
God — the Bible — He is telling you that getting into the
FLOOD STAGE of God's **spiritual, emotional, physical,** and
financial blessings is God's highest wish for your life (III John
2).

Whenever you read Jesus' words, put yourself into the
position that He is talking to *you*. I know from years of personal experience that as you read His words and visualize Him
talking to you, you will feel that He IS talking directly to you.
When you hear Jesus' words inside you, the main thing to do
is work at developing *a listening heart*, not merely an intellec-
tual state of mind, so you can really hear what He is saying to
you.

For example, if you get quiet and listen with your heart,

you will understand that God wants you to personally know His Son . . . THE NOW JESUS . . . and to start experiencing a NOW FLOOD-STAGE Christian life. Nothing less than GOD'S FLOOD STAGE can carry you through the problems and needs you face every day of your life.

My question was, what if you and the Lord Jesus were talking? I said this because I know beyond a doubt that . . .

> Jesus is here now, and very close to you.
>
> Jesus is speaking to you now so that you can hear Him.
>
> Jesus is telling you that miracles are actually coming toward you now!
>
> Jesus is also telling you that these miracles are coming *toward* you or *past* you and you must put yourself in a position to EXPECT A MIRACLE so you can receive it.

Jesus tells you that you are NOT a helpless, hopeless person, that there are things He wants you TO DO, which you CAN DO, that will take you out of the trickle, out of the stream, out of the river and into the FLOOD STAGE of miracle living in the NOW of your existence.

Recently I received a letter from a man, which is typical of what people are saying to me everywhere. He wrote:

> *Brother Roberts,*
>
> *The economic situation is getting worse, and families are being pulled apart – in fact, our whole society seems to be crumbling. I've never been the type to give up, but I feel that right now I'm coming very close.*
>
> *It's terribly frustrating to never ever reach the surface, or not be able to quite make ends meet. Money I've needed for car repairs forces me to cut down on food purchases and*

People write me that they often feel beaten down, sick, lonely, and even desolate in the world. And God never intended that. God intends to supply all our needs, to enlarge our lives, to give meaning and joy to our existence. We must work with God and His system — then His system will work for us.

therapy visits to my doctor.

All these little nickel and dime problems keep piling up . . . my needs are the world's needs . . . HELP! I've got to have logical, meaningful, practical answers . . . before it's TOO LATE!

Many of us feel like this man. We feel beaten down. Some of us are sick from our heads to our feet. Some of us feel lonely and desolate in the world. And God never intended that. God intends for us to be the head and not the tail (Deuteronomy 28:13). To be above and not beneath. God intends to heal us so we can feel well. God intends to supply our financial needs so we'll not be in want. He intends to enlarge our lives and cause us not to be diminished, or feel cut off from the main stream of His supply.

This is God's plan for us — to live in the FLOOD STAGE of His blessings. This is His plan, this is His system. I want to share with you how to discover His plan and to work with His system. He says, "I am the Lord, I change not" (Malachi 3:6). God is your plan and your system; therefore, since God doesn't change, His system doesn't change. We must do the changing and work with God and His system. Then His system will work for us — and His system never fails.

If you are not aware of His system, then you are not sensitive to your miracles coming toward you. If you are not expecting a miracle to happen any moment to you, then you have not made God the *Source* System for your life. You are not spending enough time and concentration on studying God's Word, and then *listening* with your heart for His Word to speak directly to you. Maybe you have not been regularly "hearing the Word" preached by someone anointed by the Holy Spirit. It is by studying the Word, then "hearing" it preached and taught that your "faith cometh" — that is, you cause it to come forth out of your heart to go to God (Romans 10:17).

KNOW WHO GOD IS

The absolutely most important thing in your life is to KNOW WHO GOD IS, and then KNOW WHO YOU ARE IN HIM. I mean to know the truth about God, what His nature is, how He feels about you, and to be in position to RECEIVE the miracles He is constantly sending toward the POINT OF NEED in your life.

The Bible tells us that the man who doesn't know God as his Source "shall not see when good cometh" (Jeremiah 17:6). You can't afford to carelessly allow your miracles to pass you by. You are to knowingly and carefully be expecting to receive them so you can live supernaturally natural and naturally supernatural in this life.

All of God's creations have a Source — a beginning. Like the streams and rivers have a source, so do you.

If you do not know WHO GOD IS, you have no SOURCE — you have nothing solidly backed up by God's Word to go back to, nothing to stand on when the going gets rough, as it always does.

If you don't know WHO GOD IS, you certainly don't know WHO YOU ARE or who your Source is. You are like an accident going off to happen instead of a miracle about to happen.

What you are really doing is reaching out in life for something real and getting a handful of nothing instead of a handful of the *more abundant life* that Jesus personally tells you you are to have:

I am come that you might have life, and that
you might have it more abundantly (John 10:10).

In no way does Jesus want you to live less than abundantly. He said the very reason He came was that you would live

11

"more abundantly." Jesus does not lie to you but tells you the absolute truth, for He is "the Way, the Truth, and the Life" (John 14:6).

Since Jesus himself is the Truth, the Way, and the Life, He wants you to know WHO YOU ARE in Him. If you don't know WHO YOU ARE, the devil is having a field day oppressing you with the kind of financial stress, spiritual lack, and physical sickness that cannot be cured by man alone; therefore, emotional problems make you feel like you're a yo-yo — going up and down — and more down than up. That is NOT what Jesus wants you to have. If you could just sit down a little while and "have a little talk" with Him, you could know this.

The devil knows when you do not know who you are because your beginning is not in God, your SOURCE, so the devil claims you as his property. He lies to you and you believe the lie. He brings bad things upon you and you blame God for it. As you listen to the devil instead of to Jesus, he builds such a bad image of God in your mind that you are either frightened of God or you ignore Him as the most important One in your day-by-day living.

GOD TALKS DIRECTLY TO YOU

You see, when you study God's words to you in the Holy Bible and hear them preached and taught, you can actually "hear" God saying His words directly to you:

Beloved, I wish above all things that thou mayest prosper and be in health, even as thy soul prospereth (III John 2).

I am the Lord that healeth thee (Exodus 15:26).

It is [the Lord who] giveth thee power to get wealth (Deuteronomy 8:18).

Give, and it shall be given unto you: good measure, pressed down, and shaken together, and

running over, shall men give into your bosom
(Luke 6:38).

Bring ye all the tithes [and offerings] into the
storehouse . . . and prove me now herewith, saith
the Lord of hosts, if I will not open you the
windows of heaven, and pour you out a blessing,
that there shall not be room enough to receive
[contain] it. And I will rebuke the devourer
[Satan] for your sake (Malachi 3:10,11).

Whatsoever a man soweth, that shall he also
reap . . . in due season (Galatians 6:7,9).

I can do all things through Christ which
strengtheneth me (Philippians 4:13).

My God shall supply all your need according to
his riches in glory by Christ Jesus (Philippians
4:19).

There are literally hundreds and hundreds of such promises God makes to you in the Bible. In them God means what He says and says what He means. Even when I hold the Bible in my hand I have the feeling that God is near me. To open it and study it is like God and I are sitting and talking over the most important things in my life. And when I hear the Word preached or taught, my faith comes up; I feel it rising to God.

Once again, when you don't know WHO GOD IS — and through knowing Him, WHO YOU ARE — you permit the devil to steal your miracles away. Therefore, you rob yourself of the one irresistible force that settles the issue and meets the need you have.

A MIRACLE ALWAYS SETTLES THE ISSUE!

Without God's miracles, the issues in your life are in a state of never being settled. James 1:6 says that you are like "a wave of the sea driven with the wind and tossed." You may *exist*

without miracles, but you can't live *abundantly* without them
. . . in the FLOOD STAGE of God's blessings.

You must press toward understanding that God wants you
to understand His system, and as you work with His system
He will BLESS you and MAKE you a BLESSING. By learning how to bring your nature into harmony with God's nature
you become one with Him, and you discover yourself on the
road to becoming a whole person.

In order to know where you're going with your life, in order
to have a hope for the future and a faith that lifts you above
your problems, you have to get back to your faith beginnings,
your Source — God.

Now let's go all the way back to the history of God's Source
System for our lives, for truly our beginnings are in Him and
our success in life is in working with His system.

SUMMED UP

1. Visualize Jesus talking to you.
2. Develop a listening heart.
3. Know that miracles are coming toward you now!
4. God's system is for you to live in FLOOD STAGE.
5. Know who God is so you can know who you are.
6. Learn that Jesus wants you to live abundantly.
7. God's system is to *bless* you and *make* you a *blessing*.

Write down what this chapter said to you — right now.

_____

_____

_____

_____

_____

_____

_____

_____

_____

_____

_____

_____

_____

_____

CHAPTER TWO

BACK TO YOUR BEGINNINGS — KNOW WHO GOD IS AND WHO YOU ARE IN GOD

*While the earth remaineth, seedtime and harvest
. . . shall not cease.* —Genesis 8:22

THERE WAS A NEWS story a short time ago about a young woman in Florida who had lost her memory and was found wandering the streets. The news media picked up the report and ran pictures telling of the young woman's plight. Her parents recognized and identified her and went to the authorities to pick her up and take her home.

But she refused to go! She rejected her parents' claim to her because she said she just did not KNOW them!

If this young woman had recognized and known who her parents were, then she could have known who she was. You see, they knew her, but she did not know them. If she had only recognized who her parents were, then she could have begun to put her confused life back together again.

You must know your *beginnings.* You must know where you came from. For if you don't know your beginnings you can't know where you're going. You become confused and you find your life becoming the very thing you don't want: a losing battle.

I'm talking to you on the level of your deepest needs and greatest desires. I'm talking about having a touch of God that begins inside your soul and starts welling up and coming up

through your flesh and out into your life so that SPIRITU-
ALLY, PHYSICALLY, FINANCIALLY, EVERY ONE OF
YOUR NEEDS IS COVERED BY GOD'S BLESSINGS.

That's what the FLOOD STAGE of God's blessings is all
about. And that's why I believe you and I want to learn about
how we can live and dwell in this kind of abundance with our
lives. And to do this we must know our faith beginnings.

OUR FAITH BEGINNINGS

Your roots, and my roots, go all the way back to the beginning when God created the world, then created the first man,
Adam, and spoke His love and goodness to him. He gave
Adam the power to know WHO GOD IS and to talk with Him
as naturally as breathing, to have the closest fellowship with
Him, to walk together with Him in life. But Adam did not
cultivate a *listening heart*. Soon he was not paying attention
to God to hear what God was saying to him, or to understand
God's nature or to see His system and plan for his life.

Through the very power of choice God had given him,
Adam finally *chose* to turn his back on God. He *closed* his
spirit and mind to what God was saying to him and eventually
he lost his understanding of God. Instead of meditating on
God and His system, Adam meditated on himself: going his
own way and doing his own thing. Soon he and God did not
walk in fellowship together anymore. He thought he didn't
need God, that he could make it on his own. It is hard to
believe that Adam, personally created by God and who talked
with God so often, could actually rebel in his heart against His
Creator and Source, but he did.

ADAM SHUT OFF GOD'S BLESSINGS

Adam's sin, or disobedience to God, caused him to lose
paradise — Eden — that wondrous *place* and *relationship*
with God where he knew WHO GOD WAS and, therefore,

WHO HE WAS, and how to live the more abundant life on this earth. Yes, he lost. Oh! how he lost! Think of what he lost and what all we, his descendants, lost in being born with his nature in us. Yes, we are organic descendants of Adam.

As a result, Adam by his disobedience shut off his life from being *blessed* of God and being *made a blessing* to all future mankind. He also lost the original form of rulership God had given him over the earth (Genesis 1:28). Instead of having only to "dress" the garden and keep it in fertility and harmony, he had to strive to "subdue" an earth which, because of his sin, had the same curse to fall on it as had fallen on Adam. It was changed into a wild weed-growing, hard-yielding earth, filled with all kinds of destructive germs and poisons. By the *sweat of his brow* Adam and his descendants would have to eke out a living, and the birth of his children would be through great pain to the woman (Genesis 3:16-19).

We see this today all too clearly, as most of the earth is not productive at all and all human birth causes pain.

During the ten generations from Adam to Noah, mankind lived in the great *void* that had been created by Adam's rebellion. They lived as if they had *no* beginnings, or roots, tracing back to God, as if they had never, through their forefather, Adam, been connected with God at all. Their sin — the same kind of disobedience — "filled the whole earth until God was grieved that he had ever made man" (Genesis 6:5,6).

But the goodness of God was eternal, not temporary. God had made man His crowning work, His masterpiece, containing His own likeness and image, and He loved him with an everlasting love. It is important to you to know that the glory of God given to Adam still was in the earth and remained over it. Adam's rebellion had brought a curse on the earth and a terrible void, but God still existed. His Spirit continued dealing with man's spirit to get him to return to Him and to God's system and plan for his life.

WHAT THE DEVIL COULD AND COULD NOT DO

The fallen archangel, Lucifer, meaning *light bearer,* who in his rebellion against God in heaven was cast to the earth, tempted Adam through the serpent to disobey God and, through Adam's disobedience, brought sin into the world (Genesis 3:13-19).

Instead of developing a *listening heart to God,* Adam listened to the devil and believed his words instead of God's.

Jesus said, "The devil is a liar, and the father of lies" (John 8:44). The devil lied to Adam and his descendants about God, denying His goodness and making sin look better than obedience to God. Man bought that lie then and is still buying it now.

But there were some things the devil could not do.

He could not take God out of His world, or destroy man's roots, or blot out man's ability to talk with God and listen to Him IF MAN SO CHOSE. For God had given man the greatest thing of all: the power of choice.

The devil tempted Adam's descendants to sin until their sin filled the earth and God sent a flood to wipe out sinful man. But the devil could not completely erase the glory of the Creator, for God started over with righteous Noah and his family (Genesis 7:1).

So, although man's sin had caused the Flood, God still had one righteous family to begin with again.

NOAH BELIEVED GOD

Noah believed God, and as God talked with him he heard and answered God with his *listening, obedient heart.* Given orders to build the ark, a boat large enough to carry two of every living thing through the Flood, Noah obeyed.

In our language today Noah said, "Faith, come up out of my

heart. Faith, go up to God and believe that through God you can build the ark and preserve the human race." So by releasing his faith, Noah was shown by God how to build the ark for the saving of a remnant of man and God was able to defeat the devil from having all mankind perish in the Flood. All those who followed the devil went down with the Flood. But Noah's family and two of every living thing were preserved.

FAITH IS GREATER THAN THE DEVIL'S POWER

As the tiniest light pierces all the darkness in the world, so the faith Noah released to God was greater than all the devil's destructive power. And it is the same today for you and me with our faith when we, by an act of our choice, release it to God.

Having faith inside us is not enough. A man told me, "I have all the faith in the world." I said, "That's your trouble. You still have it." He said, "What do you mean?" I said, "For your faith to work you have to choose to release it, to send it to God." He thought it over and said, "Oh, I see. My faith only works when I release it and get it out of me up to God." It changed his life!

As Noah acted on his faith to build the ark and bring his family and two of every living thing into it to survive the Flood, we see that God was still active in the earth. Even though man had refused God and cast Him aside, God's presence still remained and He continued to respond to those who released their faith. Consequently, sickness was not able to take FULL root upon the earth or upon man's body, which had been so wondrously made by God.

As the Flood waters covered the earth and the ark held firm, Noah and his family, and all living things in it, survived all sickness. Imagine what it was like to be cooped up in that boat with all other living creatures and not get sick! And all came forth from the ark healthy enough to live on the earth again, each able to reproduce its own species.

Noah listened to God instead of the devil. He chose to believe God rather than the devil, to accept the authority of God's Word, and work with His system. Thus, through Noah's faith, the human race was saved from the Flood that covered the whole earth, wiping out disobedient man who in his heart had ruled God out of his life forever.

When the Flood receded and the ark settled back on the earth again, God was there. He met Noah and talked to him.

Notice that God immediately blessed Noah and his family through their roots that went back both organically and by faith to the time when God first created the world and Adam. Noah was the tenth organic descendant of Adam. But it was his faith that kept him connected to his *spiritual beginnings*, when God created man a spiritual being.

The same blessing that God had given man when He created him (Genesis 1:28) was repeated in Noah when he came forth from the ark to land:

> *And God blessed Noah and his sons, and said unto them, Be fruitful, and multiply, and replenish the earth* (Genesis 9:1). God said, *Bring forth abundantly in the earth, and multiply therein* (v. 7).

Then God gave the key to that abundance and multiplication by tying man's life to the *principle of the seed*. God told Noah that while the earth remained there would be "*seedtime* and *harvest*" (Genesis 8:22).

THE PRINCIPLE OF THE SEED

If you can get a single seed under a microscope, watch what you see. You will see God in that seed because it's alive. It will be moving, pushing, and trying to multiply itself every second. As you see that seed just bursting to multiply, realize you are looking at your faith which is straining inside you to come

Recently I held a basket of seed in my hands, the seeds overflowing onto the ground. It helped me realize again that the Seed Principle touches every part of our lives. It is the core of God's system for you and me. When you see a seed just bursting to multiply, realize you are looking at your faith which is straining inside you to come up and out.

up and out, to go up to God, who will take it in His hands and use it as the force to create His mighty supply in you for all your needs.

For you to know WHO GOD IS and WHO YOU ARE, you must understand the eternal *principle of the seed.* All your life and everything that touches your life is in the *Seed Principle.* The seed is what God works with and it is the core of His system.

When the devil led Adam into sin and the Fall that changed Adam from the way God had created him, God pronounced a curse on the devil and then promised a Deliverer. He said to the devil, "The SEED of the woman shall bruise thy head" (Genesis 3:15). This was God's promise that on the cross Jesus would begin the destruction of the devil, and Jesus would do it as the "seed" of the woman. All of life comes from a seed.

The promise of salvation for fallen man was through the "seed" of Eve. This was in reference to the coming of the Savior as the Son of a virgin, Mary, in whose womb the Holy Spirit placed the "divine seed" of Jesus' Spirit, and from her womb brought forth Jesus in His "human form" (Matthew 1:18-25).

Jesus had no earthly father, since if He had been born of a human seed, He would have been conceived in sin as the rest of mankind has been since Adam. By being the seed of God himself, placed in the womb of a virgin, Mary, the Spirit of Jesus had no sin and He was born our Savior — perfect God/ perfect man. Therefore, He became our perfect Redeemer!

Keep in mind that the SEED became the single thread of God's promise to destroy the devil and restore man (including you and me). The SEED is the redemptive force, the single most unifying force of all creation.

As God spoke to Noah, once he was on dry land again, He revealed the link between the "seed of the woman" and "seedtime and harvest" — which is the eternal principle of

SEED-FAITH. "As long as earth remaineth," God told Noah, "there will be seedtime and harvest."

Study what Jesus said about seed and our faith. He said, "If you have faith as a grain of mustard SEED, ye shall say unto this mountain, Remove hence to yonder place; and it shall remove; and nothing shall be impossible unto you" (Matthew 17:20).

It is no accident that Jesus spoke of faith in terms of a seed which is to be planted. Even if it is the smallest seed in the world, like the mustard seed, if it is planted it becomes the force that moves mountains . . . and makes all things possible to us.

One of the most powerful and effective things I ever learned is that our faith has to be released in the same way a seed has to be released by the farmer and planted for it to multiply and produce a harvest. I grew up on a farm and helped plant our crops. I know that an unplanted seed will never reproduce and multiply itself. There is no use to look for a harvest unless you FIRST plant the seed for it. In these 34 years of working with faith, I know experientially that I must release my faith to God so He will have something to work with for miracles in my life.

ABRAHAM AND THE SEED PRINCIPLE

Abraham was the first man to discover how to use the eternal principle of the seed in terms of its relationship to faith. This is one of the most important reasons Abraham's faith is "Foundation Faith" for us today. He learned to release his faith and look beyond himself and his own needs to the "Most High God." For this reason God said Abraham's faith "was accounted to him for righteousness" (Galatians 3:6). This means when God looked at Abraham's faith, He saw Abraham as though he had never sinned . . . and covered him with His own righteousness. It was by his faith that Abraham saw God as His Source and soon was living in the FLOOD STAGE OF GOD'S BLESSINGS.

Therefore it is very important for you to look at Abraham's life and learn the eternal principle of the seed which he discovered and with which he connected his faith. Then you can also enter into the FLOOD STAGE OF BLESSING WHERE YOUR NEEDS CAN BE MET.

SUMMED UP

1. Learn your beginnings.
2. God gave you the power to choose Him or the devil.
3. Disobedience shuts off God's blessings.
4. Learn what the devil can do and cannot do in your life.
5. Your faith must be released in order to work.
6. Know that your whole life is in the seed.
7. Learn the principles of Seed-Faith.
8. Your faith originates from Abraham's Foundation Faith.

*   *   *

What does this chapter say to you? Write it here, now.

_____

_____

_____

_____

_____

CHAPTER THREE

GOD IS YOUR SOURCE SYSTEM — ONE YOU CAN COUNT ON

Abraham believed in the Lord; and he counted it to him for righteousness.
— Genesis 15:6; Galatians 3:6

ABRAHAM WAS THE FIRST true SEED-FAITH man. He turned his faith into action by getting into the rhythm of God's eternal law of sowing and reaping, giving and receiving, and was BLESSED by God and then MADE A BLESSING to others. This is the kind of faith you and I have if we will only learn to use it.

Before Abraham, there were other great men of faith. But Abraham's faith outshone their faith because it was a faith that was a GIVING FAITH. The two words that characterize Abraham's faith are GIVING/LIVING. You see, the faith of those before him had been mostly used in behalf of themselves, including Noah's in the saving of his own family. But Abraham's faith WENT BEYOND HIMSELF and affected all mankind by its quality of "giving and receiving" (sowing and reaping).

ABRAHAM BELIEVED GOD

I want you to stop and carefully consider Abraham, of whom St. Paul says, "Know ye therefore that they which are of faith, the same are the children of Abraham" (Galatians 3:7).

This is one exciting statement. Abraham, of all the people

on earth, believed God and, because of his believing, was seen by God as righteous. Therefore we who have the same kind of faith are Abraham's *spiritual* sons and daughters. Our faith originated in his Foundation Faith.

Organically we descend from *Adam; spiritually,* by faith, we descend from *Abraham.* Think on that difference and how it still exists today.

WE ARE SPIRITUAL SONS AND DAUGHTERS OF ABRAHAM

We who are living by faith in God — a faith that is a knowing of God inside us — are covered spiritually by the same righteousness of God which covered Abraham. In other words, when God looks at us as we are in faith, even though we are organic descendants of Adam, He no longer sees the things we have done wrong in the past. We have repented of all those sins and by our faith God has removed them by the shed blood of His own Son on the cross. We stand today, in the NOW of our lives, righteous in the sight of God — or in right relationship with Him. Something good has happened to us . . . and continues to happen.

In Galatians 3:29, St. Paul further says, "And if ye be Christ's, then are ye Abraham's seed, and heirs according to the promise." Notice the eternal principle of the SEED is still working in us today. Because we belong to Christ we are the SEED of Abraham, and that MAKES US HEIRS to the eternal promise of blessing and multiplication that God made to Abraham: "Surely blessing I will bless thee, and multiplying I will multiply thee" (Hebrews 6:14). This is the very essence of Seed-Faith. When we release our faith to God we must think of it as a seed for God to multiply as blessings to us, and through us.

We are the descendants of Abraham, not by physical birth as our brothers the Jews are, but by our faith in God as our Source and Redeemer we have been MADE Abraham's sons and daughters spiritually. We have been "grafted" in, made "reborn" sons and daughters of Abraham, the first man to return to Foundation Faith in the Living God which Adam originally had rejected.

So our faith as Christians actually goes all the way back and connects with the Foundation Faith Abraham had, and our faith is the same *nature* as Abraham's faith. He was the first man to have faith that went beyond himself to recognize WHO GOD WAS when other men believed only in man-made gods. This was really the beginning point of faith as you and I know faith in Jesus Christ, our Savior, today. Let's see now how Abraham's faith developed.

OUR BUILT-IN DESIRE TO WORSHIP GOD

By Abraham's time, the world had put down, in their minds, the one true God and had created other gods in His place.

Why did people create these other gods? To try to satisfy their spiritual thirst.

God in creating man and making himself his Source, built something of himself within all men. He made each of us incurably religious and spiritual. We have built into our inner selves the insatiable desire — and need — to seek after Someone greater than ourselves.

This reminds me of the story about a little boy and his daddy. The father was working in the den and the little boy kept running in and out of the room. Finally, the father, who was by now a little frustrated, said, "Son, I'm really busy. What is it that you want?"

The little boy replied, "I don't want anything."

"Then, why do you keep running in and out of here?" asked the father.

"I just need to be near you, Daddy," was the boy's response.

The father gathered the boy up in his arms, hugged him close, and said, "Son, you can stay with me all day long if you want."

God has placed in every one of us that special desire to be near Him, to live in His love.

When man turned from this One greater than himself — the one true God — he still had to satisfy his all-consuming spiritual thirst. So he made other gods, or worshiped things already in the universe as gods.

Because of their built-in desire to look up to Someone greater, God their Source, people often placed substitutes — these man-made gods — on the highest places of earth, the hills and mountains, or pictured them in the solar system. They did everything possible to make these gods real as a source to them, but their efforts were futile.

The only real Source System was God and they had tried to substitute their own lifeless gods in His place (Isaiah 44:14-17).

Then there came a man among men who turned away from worshiping these substitutes of God which also included graven images. That man was Abraham. He refused to look up to or bow before these man-created images of God and worship them as the true God.

Abraham by his faith in the true God rejected the thousands of gods in the earth. He believed in the ONE God and that He was above them all. Abraham's faith saw God in *four* ways . . .

- THE MOST HIGH GOD,
- POSSESSOR OF HEAVEN AND EARTH,
- DELIVERER FROM ALL OUR ENEMIES,
- THE GOD TO WHOM HE GAVE HIS TITHES.

(Genesis 14:20)

We will be referring to these four things about Abraham's

29

faith again and again, until we know them in our heart. These are the four foundation stones of the one faith both in the Old and New Testaments. This is what St. Paul was referring to when he said, "There . . . is one faith" (Ephesians 4:4,5).

FOUNDATION FAITH BEGINS WITH GOD'S WORD

God spoke to Abraham, just as He had spoken to Adam. When Abraham heard God's voice speaking to him, he *listened* because he had cultivated a *listening* heart. Marvelous things began to happen in his life, and through his life. Abraham let God's words drill down into his thirsty spirit where his Foundation Faith was just waiting to burst forth.

I was born and raised in the oil fields of Oklahoma. As a boy in Pontotoc County when they first drilled for oil there, I watched that oil coming up out of the ground. They would erect the great wooden derricks and drill deep into the earth, and when they hit the right spot the oil would come gushing up, spouting hundreds of feet into the sky. They called this "a gusher." It was an awesome sight to a little boy.

Now the oil was there all the time. But they had to discover it and then drill for it in the earth and bring it up. This is exactly the way it is with our faith and the kind of Foundation Faith which Abraham had. The FAITH WAS THERE ALL THE TIME! But it took God's word to Abraham to drill down inside him so by faith in God's word he would bring it forth.

Abraham heard God's voice and obeyed. He believed God. Centuries later, St. Paul was to say, "Faith comes by hearing, and hearing by the word of God" (Romans 10:17). Abraham's hearing God as He spoke to him, caused Foundation Faith in God to be reestablished as the roots of our faith. It is in this Foundation Faith that it all began for you and me. And that is why Abraham's faith is so important to you and me today in the Christian era. It is faith that makes God our Source — the Source System of our lives.

The fact that people reject this Source System doesn't change God. He said, "I am the Lord, I change not" (Malachi 3:6). People are beating their brains out trying to establish their "humanism" (which is already recognized by the U.S. Supreme Court as a religion), and what does it get them? The substitution of their humanistic gods for the true God is a product of their choice and will, not God's. They, not God, have plunged this world system into chaos. We must stop blaming God for the bad things happening in the world, and put the blame where it belongs: on the devil and our taking his way over God's.

A LESSON FROM THE PEACH ORCHARD

I grew up near my Uncle Willis Roberts who owned a big orchard where he grew Elberta peaches. That's how he made his money, educated his children, and supported his family.

One day the orchard began to die. The fruit got smaller and smaller as the trees began to wither.

So Uncle Willis drove to Ada, Oklahoma, the county seat, and got an agricultural expert to come back with him to look over the orchard. And the man said, "Mr. Roberts, you have made a fatal mistake. You've taken good care of your fruit, but you haven't paid any attention to the trees. If you will take care of the trees, you won't need to worry about the fruit."

Well, I remember watching Uncle Willis uproot the trees of his orchard and replant new ones. Then years later, when I went back for a visit, I saw that new orchard thriving and producing great big Elberta peaches. And there was Uncle Willis outside tending those new trees — watering them, digging around them, spraying them.

You see, the SOURCE of that fruit was the trees and the system was in working with them. The fruit could not grow and be healthy if it was not connected to a healthy, thriving source.

Likewise, we must know that every human weakness, by birth or by that which happens after birth, originated *organically* from Adam's sin of rejecting God as his Source, plunging him and his descendants into the hand of the devil with his disease-bringing, death-dealing forces of human destruction.

You can get your thoughts straightened out on that by studying God's Holy Word for yourself. The Bible holds all the answers. It tells us who God is, who we are, where we came from, and where we are going. And it tells us about faith, which is our "straight line to God," to reject the devil and put us in the FLOOD STAGE of God's blessings spiritually, physically, and financially.

YOUR FAITH IS THE STRAIGHT LINE TO YOUR SOURCE

Your faith becomes your straight line to God. Isn't this what you and I really need for our lives? A "faith seed" we plant that connects us directly with our Source?

If you cut a stream off from the mountain springs that issue forth water, it will dry up. Without that source of water there can never be a stream. There can never be a flowing river. There can never be a limitless flood without a source from which the water will flow.

That's the way it is with our lives in relation to God as our Source. Before we can ever begin to get into the FLOOD STAGE of God's blessings, we must first recognize and know who our Source is and what His system is. We must have a channel — a straight line — between us and God, and this comes through learning how to use our faith.

In order for you to have God's full and overflowing blessings on your life, it is very important for us to talk about Abraham's faith, the faith that St. Paul said we must have to be sons and daughters of God.

SUMMED UP

1. When you believe God, He covers you with His righteousness.
2. Through your faith you are a son or daughter of Abraham.
3. Learn the eternal principle of the seed.
4. You have a built-in desire to worship God.
5. You can learn to bring your faith up to God.
6. Get a Source for your life.
7. Learn about Abraham's faith as it applies to you today.

* * *

What does this chapter say to you? Write it down.

_____

_____

_____

_____

_____

_____

_____

_____

_____

CHAPTER FOUR

ABRAHAM'S STRUGGLE OF FAITH . . . YOUR EXAMPLE TO GET INTO FLOOD STAGE LIVING

[Abraham] against hope believed in hope, that he might become the father of many nations, according to that which was spoken [promised].
—Romans 4:18

As YOU READ HOW Abraham was blessed by using his faith, you may find yourself saying, "But that was Abraham. He was a man of GREAT FAITH. My faith isn't that great. I have only a little faith."

Hold it right there! What you are saying may be the greatest discovery you will ever make. You may be right. You may have only a "little faith," but FAITH IS FAITH JUST LIKE GOLD IS GOLD. FAITH IS FAITH WHEREVER YOU FIND IT. IT'S STILL FAITH!

Let us not make the mistake of looking at Abraham only AFTER his faith had developed to the point where he knew WHO GOD WAS and therefore WHO HE WAS, and began joyously giving tithes of all.

Let us look at those times before this happened when God was just a word to him, and to those around him a byword or curse word. Abraham did not always have the *developed* kind of faith. He had to begin in faith the same way we do. In Hebrews 12:2 we are told to be in a state of "looking unto Jesus, the author and finisher of our faith." This shows us that there is a *beginning* of our faith and a *developing* of our faith.

You see, Abraham's family did not know the true God, so they were worshipers of man-made gods. Built into them like everyone else was the desire to worship God. Since they didn't know WHO GOD WAS, they had a poor self-image and descended to the place where they put their trust in *things* rather than God. Therefore, they had no true Source as Abraham was to discover for himself years later.

GREAT FAITH HAS TO BE DEVELOPED

I think one of the faults we Christians have is that we read about people in the Bible who had faith and we're tempted to make "instant" saints out of them, or to look at them only after they worked at their faith, continually learning how to release it to God in good times and bad.

We must be more realistic than this or we will never understand that our own faith has to "start," and our faith has to be "developed" — by us. And that happens by constantly releasing it over a period of time, usually over a number of years.

Speaking personally, I know that because I am human, the releasing of my faith is always a *struggle.* I do not recall a time when it was easy to "turn my faith loose." It has always meant going against the current of men's opinions, of the devil's opposition, of my own humanness, or of not understanding God's system. However, I find that the more I work at believing God, reaching up to Him more and more, the better I can do it. And I don't believe it will be any different for you.

Now let's take a close, careful look at Abraham's continuous struggle of faith, with emphasis on his *struggle.*

First, his family were not believers originally. That was a struggle he had to rise over, not once, not twice, but continuously.

Second, when he began to hear God speaking inside him (as we all do in some way), and he understood that he was to get up and leave his people, he just couldn't summon the faith and courage to do it for some time. It was a struggle. Finally, when he did get strong enough to start the trip, he discovered his father and a few others chose to go with him, but he couldn't even tell them where God wanted him to go. That was really a struggle to his mind when he said, "I don't even know exactly where God wants me to go." Therefore, before the journey was over, his folks talked him into stopping. While at one of the places — Haran — he lost his father (Genesis 11:32). No doubt, that tempted him to turn back instead of going on, trusting his faith in God that he would eventually get there.

Third, he married a beautiful girl but he discovered she was barren, a condition in those days that was considered to be almost a curse. Children were valued highly. Because of his wife's barrenness, Abraham realized he would have no heir. His line would stop with him. There would have been no Israel, no Christians! Talk about struggle, it was continuous struggle for Abraham.

Fourth, when he finally reached the place God had called "The Land of Promise," the place He would give to Abraham and his descendants forever, another problem came up. Abraham was told to "walk out the land" and wherever his feet touched, the land would be his and his seed's after him (Genesis 13:17).

Well, how do you think he felt when he realized his wife Sarah would never bear his seed? Also, how do you think he felt when he saw a desert land on one side and rocky hillsides and mountains on the other? There were no surveyors; he literally had been told to walk out the land, just as it was.

IT WASN'T EASY TO HAVE FAITH

Talk about being lonely, becoming disillusioned, getting depressed over what you have been promised, your mind reeling at what seems so absurd and impossible, your body getting so tired you can hardly move — well, Abraham went through all these experiences, and more, in the *PROCESS of developing the faith he had and RELEASING it to God.*

Man-made gods were everywhere. People mocked every time there was mention of a man named Abraham, who believed he was made in God's likeness and was, therefore, a spiritual being living in a physical body. Also, they mocked when he "gave tithes of all" to a God he couldn't even see. Talk about us being thought of as strange, what would people think of Abraham if he lived in our day? If we are walking in the steps of his faith, as St. Paul said in Romans 4:12, you can be sure people *are* talking about us! And sometimes mocking us. We too struggle to develop our faith and to release it.

Stories were being told of a flood only ten generations before Abraham in which only one family in all the earth — Noah's — was spared. By then people were ridiculing such a story, and they are still trying to get us to reject the fact of the Flood today.

Also, the one language God had originally given Adam had been shattered into hundreds of dialects and tongues. Only recently in Abraham's time had this happened. Nimrod, a man who hated the name of God, became a "mighty hunter" of men who believed in God. He sought to destroy them and to destroy the name of God from the earth (Genesis 10:9). Nimrod was the first man to become a world dictator!

Because all men still spoke the one language given to Adam, it was easy for Nimrod to communicate in that one language his ambitions of building a tower to heaven. He and many others had so usurped God's power that they believed *they* possessed the earth and now they wanted to build a tower to heaven so they could possess heaven, too.

God had created man with such powers that He said of them. ". . . and now nothing will be restrained from them, which they have imagined to do" (Genesis 11:6).

So God shattered their language because He had placed in human speech the ability to articulate or express a person's spiritual, mental, and physical powers. The group at Babel had this oneness of thought in their speech against God, and also had the conceptual ability to pervert His ownership of all things. Also, Satan had such a stronghold on them that their effort to reach heaven was actually an all-out satanic war against heaven itself.

God had to stop them. We read in Genesis 11:7,8:

> Go to, let us go down, and there confound their
> language, that they may not understand one
> another's speech. So the Lord scattered them
> abroad from thence upon the face of all the earth:
> and they left off to build the city.

By Abraham's time man, by the shattering of his language at Babel, had broken off into many different languages, cultures, and religious groups and had found his place in different parts of the earth. This is the way racial and national barriers came into being. Each had only a fragment of the original language, as is so tragically true today.

GOD STARTED OVER WITH ONE MAN

Can you imagine the fun they poked at Abraham as they saw him "walking out the land," seemingly aimlessly, over the deserts and mountains of the land that would become Israel — his feet blistered, his wife unable to have children, yet that man struggling to hold on to his sanity and believe God would guide him? A man alone and dreaming God's dream — a dream to start over with ONE man who would have faith, and through him build a Chosen People out of whom the Promised Redeemer — the seed of the woman promised at Adam's fall in Genesis 3:15 — would come?

Demonic power was everywhere. Raw heathenism was

rampant. The world was being populated by these different language and cultural groups, each not understanding the other, and soon the world was an armed camp.

No, it wasn't easy to have faith. It never has been; it never will be; it is always a struggle.

The judgment at Babel ended God's trying again to work with the WHOLE of mankind. He was now attempting to start over with ONE man. Hopefully from this ONE man's faith He could heal Sarah's womb, giving Abraham a son out of whom a nation of faith-people would rise — Israel — and out of Israel a Savior, Jesus Christ, who would become our Savior and Lord; and through Him God would love and woo all mankind to return to Him (John 3:16).

THE MIRACLE OF GOD'S FAITH IN US

Talk about faith and how hard it seems for us to have it, then *consider the faith God has in us.* With everything He had attempted through creation now down to ONE man, God believed this man Abraham would have faith and obey Him, dreaming not his own dream but God's. Now that's faith!

A man said to me, "Oral, my problem is I just can't believe in God." I replied, "That's not my problem. Mine is to believe that He can believe in me."

And I really mean that. God didn't have much to start with when He came into my broken life — my body racked with tuberculosis, my tongue unable to talk without stuttering, and what little promise of life I had being defeated, not only by affliction but by my own disobedience.

Even after I started believing God to save my soul and heal my body, it was hard to believe I would ever amount to anything. Called to the ministry of healing, my faith was so small I went 12 years after my conversion and healing without attempting to pray for the sick, except in rare instances. And when I began praying for the sick with the full force of my

39

faith in 1947, the forces of Satan were released against me by some of my closest friends to cause people to believe I was in it only for the money, and not because I cared that people would come into health and wholeness. That was one reason I made the vow, "I will touch neither the gold nor the glory." That vow I have kept to this hour.

I felt so inadequate! And I wondered if God would heal enough people through my preaching and praying that even a small impression would be made on mankind to know God is a healing God. My obedience to God and my faith in Him began with struggle; it is still a struggle today, and in many ways a deeper struggle.

I ALMOST LOST MY HEALING

In fact, after my healing I almost lost it before I could share it with someone else. The healing touch upon my lungs was instant, but the renewing of strength to my wasted body was very slow, taking almost a year to get strong again.

One day Mamma said, "Oral, you are discouraged, aren't you?"

"Yes, I am, Mamma," I replied.

"Oral, don't doubt your healing. Remember how you felt the healing of God go into your lungs, and how you rejoiced that you were being healed?"

"Mamma, I remember that, but why am I so weak? Why do I have to lie down some every day?"

There was a hurt look in Mamma's eyes, then a fierce determination. She said, "Oral, during the day it's all right to lie down across the bed and rest but do it with your clothes on. Don't get into your pajamas and under the covers, for then you might accept tuberculosis again. The disease is gone, Oral. You just need to rest some, then do some physical work until your strength comes again."

What an impression her words made on my struggling faith!

Especially that as I rested during the day I was to be careful NOT to get UNDER the bed covers. As long as I lay across the bed, fully clothed, that meant to her, and to me, my weakness was temporary instead of permanent.

FLOOD STAGE FAITH WORKS THROUGH OBEDIENCE

Mamma helped my faith to grow by talking to me about obeying God. One of the greatest things she said was, "Oral, always obey God and He will bless the world through you."

Today the students and faculty of Oral Roberts University, the prayer partners and medical staff of the City of Faith Medical and Research Center, and partners and visitors look at all the visible manifestations of faith in God which are the result of my faith and the faith of those who work with me in this ministry. They have little or no idea of the hard and lonely road of getting to this point of merging God's healing streams of prayer and medicine and of ultimately sending hundreds of missionary Healing Teams to the nations.

I am reminded of what a friend said to me once: "Oral, you can't get something out without putting something in." So when asked how all these things have been done, I reply, "You never get something for nothing. Everything you see in this ministry was begun by first planting a seed of faith as a few others and I emptied our billfolds and laid what we had on the table, prayed over it, and started digging holes for the buildings. We made contracts solely on faith since we never had the money when we started, and not always the full plans."

I can truthfully say that I have never begun anything for God without first planting a seed of my faith, then continuing to plant more seed. Through these seeds, the miracle harvests began to come which also gave me more seeds to plant. The principle of the seed is more than a principle. To me, it is the living, pulsating heart of my faith in action!

Aerial view of Oral Roberts University campus and the City of Faith in Tulsa, Oklahoma

I can truthfully say that I have never begun anything for God without first planting a seed of my faith, then continuing to plant more seed. Everything you see in this ministry was begun by first planting a seed of faith as a few others and I emptied our billfolds and laid what we had on the table, prayed over it, and started digging holes for the buildings. We made contracts solely on faith since we never had the money when we started, and not always the full plans. But as we continued planting our seeds of faith, we saw building rise up and the work of God leap into a new dimension. (Shown are some of those main buildings on the ORU campus.)

The Prayer Tower (left), where we receive almost 2,000 phone calls a day for prayer; Christ's Chapel (right), where faculty and students attend chapel services twice weekly (inset).

The Learning Resources Center, containing 14 acres of floor space. It houses the library and our seven graduate schools of medicine, dentistry, nursing, law, business, theology, and education.

The magnificent Mabee Center where convocations, athletic events, and events for the Tulsa community are held. Attached, on the left, is "Baby Mabee" where our weekly television programs and prime-time specials are taped for national and world distribution.

I often urge people not to look at my faith today, which by constant use grows stronger all the time to overcome the devil's opposition and get things done for God. I encourage them to think on these critical times when I am dreaming God's dream without knowing any possible way I can ever accomplish any of it except by planting a seed, no matter how small, no matter how much the struggle.

Faith, obedience, hard work, the willingness to be opposed and laughed at, to give God my best — planting my seeds of faith out of my deepest needs, then to expect to receive His best — these are the things I know, and the only things I know which work miracles of deliverance.

It's still not easy to pick up a newspaper or turn on the TV and see myself being held up to ridicule and scorn, while others who don't believe in a God of miracles are praised. It's still hard not to strike back. It's still lonely to announce a big new project God has laid on my heart and have to "walk out the land" by faith alone, hurting in every fiber of my being as I first plant the seed and, without seeing the miracle harvest until later — often much later — but looking for it, expecting to receive it in God's "due season."

No, nothing has changed about Abraham's faith, or about my faith or your faith as we practice GIVING/LIVING through Seed-Faith in today's mocking world. But God has said, "The just shall live by faith" (Habakkuk 2:4; Romans 1:17; Galatians 3:11; Hebrews 10:38).

Why does God tell us that we must live by our faith?

Because as difficult as it is to go against the devil to believe God, you can't afford to go against God to believe the devil. And as precarious and uncertain as it seems at times to look only to God as your Source System, your Financial System, and your Blessing System, it is absolutely futile and fatal to look to this world's system. Living by our personal faith in

God through the seeds of faith we plant is the ONLY way we can rise above the world's opposition and REALLY LIVE!

THE MIRACLE OF FAITH — EVEN "LITTLE FAITH"

Don't despise "little faith." Peter walked on the water with little faith (Matthew 14:29). The disciples went through a death-bringing storm with only a small amount of faith (Mark 4:40). A father's cry for Jesus to "help thou mine unbelief" brought healing to his little afflicted son (Mark 9:24).

Don't be afraid to launch forth for God when you don't have all of the plan or the full details but you do have a knowing in your heart. Just be sure you don't expect something for nothing, and always plant the first seed, giving it out of your need and making it best seed.

Everything I am doing for God today was first just a fragment of an idea, but an idea that wouldn't go away. When it became a "knowing" in my heart that I was to do it for God, I waited until I knew that I knew that I knew. This knowing made me realize what God put in my heart was of faith, then was to become an act of my faith. At that point I discovered that . . .

> if I "Seed-Faithed" toward that project with
> what little I had,
> if I stumbled but got up again,
> if I failed but refused to quit,

God would put it all together bit by bit, and "no weapon formed against me would prosper" (Isaiah 54:17).

I am reminded of a little boy who had a part in a church play in which he had only one line to say from the Bible. "It is I; be not afraid." He rehearsed until he had it perfectly. But on the day of the play, when they gave him his cue and he stepped out on the brightly lighted stage and saw all the people, he froze.

From behind the curtain the prompter whispered, "It is I; be not afraid."

He just stood there, shifting from foot to foot.

Again came the voice, "It is I; be not afraid."

The little boy blurted out, "Folks, it's only me and I'm scared to death!"

Well, Abraham was scared too. Knowing he was utterly alone there on the world's stage, knowing only God's promise and not the deed, opposed on every side, he started *where* he was and *as* he was and God called it *faith* and made him the "father of all who have faith," even today (Romans 4:16). You and I can take great encouragement from the faith struggles and faith accomplishments of this man Abraham.

WATERMELONS TAKE TIME AND SO DOES YOUR FAITH

I want to emphasize to you that you do not get where you are going to go overnight. The development of your faith takes an act of your will to believe God. It takes effort to believe when there seems to be no way, and it often takes time. In fact, I personally know that my believing God is a continuous effort on my part.

We are often as impatient as the little boy who saw a beautiful picture of a watermelon on a package of seeds. He bought the seeds and rushed home and opened the package. To his disappointment, no melons were inside.

His grandfather explained that seeds have to be planted to produce melons. So the little boy ran to the yard, dug a hole, and placed the seeds in the ground. Early the next morning he eagerly checked his garden. He dug down and found the seeds he had planted — but no melons. His grandfather explained that it takes time for seeds to produce melons, and that every time he dug up the seeds he delayed the harvest.

We know that about natural seeds, but we sometimes forget that the same principle is true with our seeds of faith. As you use the faith you possess, however little it is, it will grow in your heart.

As you become obedient to God's will, and then open up and release your faith to Him, you will soon find yourself living "by faith" the same as Abraham did and as all have done who obeyed God and saw "good success" (Joshua 1:8).

God wants you to have good success. That's why He has made it possible and practical for you to use your faith to produce the works of good success.

SUMMED UP

1. Don't be discouraged if you feel you have only a "little faith." Faith is faith like gold is gold.

2. As you develop whatever faith you have, it will grow.

3. The chief thing to remember is that because you are human, faith is a struggle — and faith is developed through struggle as we see in Abraham, "the father of all who have faith."

4. God started over with one man's faith — Abraham's. Although you are one person, God will work His wonders through your faith.

5. When I almost lost my healing, Mamma encouraged my faith.

6. Your faith is in GIVING/LIVING.

7. Always start everything by planting a seed. Plant it first. Plant it out of your best, and plant it out of your need.

8. God gave you faith to use because He wants you to have good success.

What does this chapter say to you? Write it down.

_____

_____

_____

_____

_____

_____

_____

_____

_____

_____

_____

_____

_____

_____

_____

_____

_____

_____

_____

_____

CHAPTER FIVE

WHY ABRAHAM'S FAITH IS IMPORTANT TO YOU TODAY

*Know ye therefore that they which are of faith,
the same are the children of Abraham.*
—Galatians 3:7

AS WE GO INTO this chapter of why Abraham's faith is so very important to you, you may be wondering why I don't cut across the Old Testament and get directly to Jesus' teaching on faith. The reason is that for your faith to work miracles, and keep on working miracles, you have to enter faith at its foundation point the same way Jesus did, which is Abraham's faith. If you miss connecting up your faith at its point of origin, you will miss miracle after miracle.

I have discovered in dealing with uncounted numbers of people, including Christian after Christian, that most seem to think there is one kind of faith in the Old Testament as it worked in Abraham, and an entirely different kind of faith in the New Testament as it worked in Jesus and His followers. Too long people have thought there are two faiths when there is only one.

St. Paul said, "There is one faith . . ." (Ephesians 4:5). Not two, but one. "They which be of faith are blessed with faithful Abraham" (Galatians 3:9). In verse 7, St. Paul said, "They which are of faith, the same are the children of Abraham." He added, "That the blessing of Abraham might come on the Gentiles through Jesus Christ . . ." (v. 14).

What is the blessing of Abraham that is upon all of us who are in Jesus Christ? God said, "And blessing I will bless thee and multiplying I will multiply thee" (Genesis 22:17; Hebrews 6:13,14).

Read Hebrews 11, the great faith chapter, and you will see faith is faith wherever you find it in God's dealings with man. In verse 6 we are told, "He that cometh to God must believe that [God] is, and that he is a rewarder of them that diligently seek him."

This is the same faith the Virgin Mary had to give birth to Jesus Christ our Savior, the same faith Jesus had in His life and ministry. When the Apostle Philip asked Jesus, "Show us the Father," Jesus answered, "He that hath seen me hath seen the Father" (John 14:8,9).

One of the reasons Jesus came in the flesh was to walk among men and do the works of the Father in order to show us WHO GOD IS and WHAT GOD IS LIKE.

I hope you will grasp afresh that the ONE FAITH St. Paul referred to in the New Testament — which is the faith all of us have who are "in Christ" — comes directly from the Foundation Faith of Abraham. It was this faith — this one faith in the true God — that runs all through the Word of God. In the Old Testament it pointed to the coming of Jesus Christ; in the New Testament it points back to Abraham's faith. It is the same MIRACLE-WORKING faith.

Abraham's faith is all-important to you and me today because he believed that God was his Source. He based that on four things he believed about God:

1. GOD IS MOST HIGH GOD
2. POSSESSOR OF HEAVEN AND EARTH
3. DELIVERER FROM ALL OUR ENEMIES
4. HE IS THE ONE WHO MULTIPLIES OUR SEED . . . SO HE GAVE TITHES OF ALL

(Genesis 14:19,20)

I hope you can see what it means for Abraham to come to know WHO GOD WAS, for it is the biblical view that Jesus presented of what God is really like. Man's view puts man first and prevents him from knowing who he is because he can never know who he is until he knows WHO GOD IS, then gives tithes of all to Him as the supreme act of his worship. Abraham's view puts God first and recognizes Him as the Source System for his life and for all his descendants who would follow in the steps of his faith (Galatians 3:7).

ABRAHAM LEARNS TO PLANT SEEDS OF FAITH

In Genesis 14 we read how Abraham's nephew Lot and his family, who lived in the ungodly city of Sodom, with the king and people of Sodom, were captured and carried far away by an enemy army.

Now Abraham and Lot had parted ways sometime before this. They had chosen to go separate paths and to live different life-styles. But when Abraham heard of Lot's dilemma, he mounted up with 318 of his men and pursued the captors.

What a mighty seed of faith Abraham was planting! Even though he was outnumbered many times, he was able through his faith in the Living God to overcome the enemy and return his kinfolk to safety. It was a seed of great love.

When Abraham returned in victory he was met by Melchizedek, the priest of God. We read from Genesis 14:18-20:

> *And Melchizedek king of Salem brought forth*
> *bread and wine; and he was the priest of the most*
> *high God. And he blessed him, and said, Blessed*
> *be Abram of the most high God, possessor of*
> *heaven and earth; and blessed be the most high*
> *God, which hath delivered thine enemies into thy*
> *hand. And he gave tithes of all.*

Notice when Abraham returned from his great victory through God his Source, two most important things happened which still happen to us today when through Christ our Savior we act as "faith" sons and daughters of Abraham:

First: Abraham was BLESSED when Melchizedek, the priest of the Most High God, pronounced a BLESSING UPON HIS LIFE.

Second: Abraham was MADE A BLESSING and he became the first man to give TITHES OF ALL to the priest of God.

In this scene we see again the NATURE of God, and the NATURE of Abraham's faith in God, which was giving, and giving first. We also see the NATURE of being BLESSED and MADE a BLESSING. The nature runs true like a crystal stream ever after.

> Right here is the *foundation* of our faith in God, from Abraham to Israel, to us today who are "in Christ." Only as there is a strong foundation can a strong house be built. It was from this foundation that the "House of Israel" was established (Ruth 4:11), out of Israel the "House of David" was established (II Samuel 7:26), and out of David, Christ was born and the "household of faith" of Christians was established (Luke 1:69; Galatians 6:10).

ABRAHAM DISCOVERS GOD'S FINANCIAL SYSTEM

Now why did Abraham give tithes of all, not only a tenth of his money but of all he possessed on earth? When he saw how great God is — that He possesses everything, that He delivers us from all our enemies, and that everything God is and has was available to him — such love and gratitude filled his heart that he wanted to give "tithes of everything." As long as he knew who God was, then who he himself was, he could not help but "give" his best to his God. This is the system God established and when we work with it, it works every time.

In his giving "tithes of all," Abraham discovered the goodness of God. He discovered that he could not outgive God. God always multiplied Abraham's seed giving and returned more to him than he gave, and Abraham's *blessed* life proved that he lived in FLOOD STAGE. When he had finished his life and looked back he saw that "the Lord had blessed him in all things" (Genesis 24:1). In Genesis 14:19,20 we see Abraham "giving tithes of all." In Genesis 24:1, years and years later, God had given him all.

Many Christians have missed "giving tithes of all," and because of it have suffered grievous loss in reaping God's harvests in every area of their lives: spiritually, physically, financially. They have floundered in confusion about why God doesn't supply their needs and put them into FLOOD STAGE. Even pastors of churches often feel uncomfortable in giving the people an opportunity to worship God in a more effective way by the "cheerful giving" of their tithes and offerings as Seed-Faith. Thank God, that is beginning to change. Now, instead of many believers cringing any time the seeding of money is mentioned in connection with worshiping God, more and more of us are coming into . . .

THE JOY OF GIVING/LIVING

St. Paul wrote, "God loveth a cheerful giver" (II Corinthians 9:7). And it is true. St. Paul knew God's basic law: when you give, receiving follows. That creates the desire to give, the cheerfulness to give, and increases God's love in us.

So many say, "But Oral Roberts, I don't expect to receive anything back from my giving." I reply, "Then you are breaking with God's basic system, and you are letting the devil steal your receiving. Because you are NOT expecting to reap from the seed you have planted to God, you are suffering LACK, WANT, AND DOUBT THAT GOD IS A GOOD GOD."

There are three things about giving that stand out to me in

God's system, and as I see GIVING/LIVING work today:

1. A rejected opportunity to give is a lost opportunity to receive.
2. Being neutral about the opportunity to give neutralizes the flow of what God wants to give to you.
3. An accepted opportunity to give is an accepted opportunity to receive. This is the very heart of seedtime and harvest which I call Seed-Faith.

I can't tell you how many people have told me how grateful they are that I shared God's system of joyous giving and receiving with them and they started right in to give, then to expect to receive their miracle-harvest . . . and they are receiving!

I was born the son of an Oklahoma sharecropper and worked as a farm boy (later Papa became a minister of the gospel). Papa constantly talked about the harvest, which taught me the benefits of planting. If we did not plant first, we wouldn't have a harvest to reap. Mamma helped my faith to grow by talking to me about obeying God. The greatest thing she said to me was, "Oral, always obey God and He will bless the world through you."

PAPA AND OUR COTTON CROP

I am glad the Bible compares our giving and receiving to sowing and reaping, because since I was born the son of an Oklahoma sharecropper and worked as a farm boy, I understand the principles involved.

Our main crop was cotton. I entered the hard work of helping Papa plant because I knew it was the only way a cotton crop could be grown. I knew this was our money crop and it would feed, clothe, and keep us warm in the winter months. Even though I knew this, Papa had a hard time getting me excited about planting the cotton seeds! What he did was to tell me about all we were going to receive from all the planting we were doing. He constantly talked about the harvest which showed me the benefits of planting.

You may have had a hard time getting excited about *giving* because you did not know that you are to expect God's miracle harvest back.

YOU SOW IT, GOD GROWS IT, AND YOU REAP IT

When you give to God, you're not giving something away, because what you give is a SEED SOWN:

Galatians 6:7 says from THAT you "shall reap." God must return that seed to you multiplied . . . and running over (II Corinthians 9:10; Luke 6:38). In both the Old and New Testaments, this is God's infallible system through which He increases our seed sown and at the same time increases our righteousness before Him.

Here is how St. Paul, in Galatians 6:7, says it in our words: You SOW it, God GROWS it, and you REAP it! Verse 9 of Galatians 6 tells us that after we SOW it and God GROWS it, there is a DUE SEASON for us to REAP it. Faith, the faith that goes back to Abraham's faith, is the key we use today to wait for God's "due season" for our miracle harvest after we sow, for the TIME and the METHOD of our receiving, as always, are in His hands. We must TRUST God for our *reaping time* in the same way we TRUST Him for our *time of sowing . . . our giving.* It is truly Seed-Faith! (I would like to confess I have tried to tell God how to give me my "due season," when and where to do it. But He never has done it exactly like I asked. He has done it His way. Maybe some day I will learn.)

The most encouraging thing for me in this world of wild confusion and constant uncertainty is that I know God will GROW what I SOW and that by looking to Him as my Source for my harvests, there is always a divinely timed "due season" for me to receive. As surely as I sow in the "good soil" of the gospel of Jesus Christ, just as surely I will reap in "due season." I have to use my faith to sow, I have to use my faith to wait on God's "due season," then reap my harvest. The same is true for you.

Let me tell you it thrills God to have us, His people, follow the faith of Abraham and to give tithes of everything we earn and possess. He knows it connects us to the blessing of Abraham, where God says: "Surely blessing I will bless thee, and multiplying I will multiply thee" (Genesis 22:17; Hebrews 6:14). The blessing of Abraham is the same in the Old Testament and in the New Testament. I cannot stress too much that the blessings of Abraham continue into the New Testament and are ours today if we act in faith.

A GLIMPSE OF GOD LEADS YOU INTO GIVING/LIVING

Look again at Abraham. Take a good look. He sees that God is highest of all. That God literally possesses heaven AND earth and all they contain, and has delivered him from every enemy, no matter how many or how strong. Abraham got a glimpse of how great, how good God is. His love for God overflowed his heart and all his possessions. He wanted to worship God with all he was and with everything he had. In a supreme act of worship of the true God, he actually could not help but "give tithes of all," knowing in his heart he could never OUTGIVE the MOST HIGH GOD, POSSESSOR OF HEAVEN AND EARTH, AND DELIVERER FROM ALL HIS ENEMIES.

This glimpse of God that Abraham had, led into GIVING/LIVING which he followed from that day for the rest of his life, and commanded it to his descendants. God said, "I know Abraham will command his children after him" (Genesis 18:19).

I GOT TURNED ON TO TITHING

When I lay dying with tuberculosis, not knowing if God cared, I got turned on to God by my sister Jewel. She said, "Oral, God is going to heal you."

This is not unlike God saying to Abraham, "I will deliver you from all your enemies because I am the Most High God and Possessor of heaven and earth, the supernatural and the natural."

Never before had I thought of God as Healer, Deliverer, Restorer of life. I had been told wrong things by many who visited my bedside, "God put this on you." "God has tracked you down." "God is punishing you."

Therefore, when my parents urged me to pray to God, I was so full of wrong thinking about Him that I had NO desire to pray to Him. He scared me.

But one night as Papa knelt at the foot of my bed praying for me, Jewel's seven miracle words began to open me up, and something marvelous happened. I glanced across my body into Papa's face and suddenly I had a GLIMPSE OF JESUS. A radiance came into Papa's face that appeared to be a flash of the face of Jesus. A flood of God's love engulfed me and, instantly, I wanted to give my heart and life to God. I wanted to give Him everything! I accepted Him that night as my personal Savior and Lord and shortly afterward my healing began.

The first thing I did was ask Mamma to get the few dollars I had previously earned and take the tithe (a tenth) and give it to God's work. God's love overflowed my heart. I saw He was greater than all my sins and all the disease I was suffering. In other words, although I did not know how to express it at that time, I really was beginning to understand that God was Most High God to me and Deliverer from my enemies. In my case, my enemy was tuberculosis.

I remember what a thrill it was to know I had become a tither! Somehow in my spirit I knew that everything God had was available to me from that hour. To be honest, I couldn't help but give even though I had only a little.

God began to bless me through my giving. Today I believe I am one of the happiest givers — Seed Faithers — in all Christendom! Why? I've found it works! The GIVING/LIVING faith of Abraham and of Jesus has become mine, too.

Why are more and more people joyously giving tithes of all? Perhaps they have begun to see God as Abraham first saw Him. Or perhaps it's because, as I have stated, many ministers are overcoming their unscriptural reluctance to teach their people the joys of "giving and receiving" as taught by St. Paul in Philippians 4:15, and of GIVING/LIVING, as their minds are opened to the faith of Abraham. I know this: it causes God to open the windows of heaven to them. It is a primary reason why so many more Christians are at last getting into FLOOD STAGE! (Malachi 3:10,11).

We who believe in Jesus as our personal Savior are of the faith of Abraham, and because of it we have a great need to know what Abraham knew about God, which caused him to give his tithes and offerings to the Lord, to give them as a supreme act of his worship, and to see God multiply them "exceedingly."

Again, let me point out to you that Abraham "gave tithes of all" because he recognized and confessed the four most important things about God and His nature:

> *The Lord is the Most High God.*
>> His name is above every name, as it is embodied in Christ the Lord today.
>
> *He is Possessor of heaven and earth.*
>> The supernatural and natural.
>
> *He is the Deliverer from all our enemies.*
>> Spiritual, physical, financial.
>
> *He is the Multiplier of our tithes given as seed to Him.*

Abraham had been believing God and separating himself from all man-made gods. But he had not reached the place in his faith that he understood those all-important four things about God. Then there came the moment of dawning, a revelation of God to his spirit of God's very nature . . . and the system He had established for His people *for all time.*

As a result, the clouds lifted, the dawn broke, and suddenly Abraham saw in God his Source System. His Financial Deliverer. Multiplier. Blesser. He saw that God is a good God, and is always a good God.

> I believe this is when the vision of Jesus and Jesus' day came to his spiritual sight and he began to be glad and rejoice. Abraham saw Jesus long before we Christians did and believed in Him. This is why Abraham's faith is our Foundation Faith. I know that many years later Jesus looked back to that time when Abraham's faith had leaped the centuries and saw Him, for He specifically referred to it: "Abraham saw my day . . . and was glad" (John 8:56). Before Jesus was born in Bethle-

hem, Judea, Abraham saw Him as Son of the Living God. How did he see Him? With the eyes of his faith!

FIRSTFRUITS GIVING

When Abraham saw WHO GOD WAS, he saw WHO HE WAS, and it caused him to open up his whole being and all his possessions to "give tithes of all."

Many people believe that tithing was instituted by the Law of Moses. That is not true. Abraham gave tithes over 400 years before Moses received the Law and followed Abraham's example by instituting tithing for the children of Israel, saying, "The tithe is the Lord's" (Leviticus 27:30).

Tithing became a *"firstfruits giving"* to God as a part of the Law of Moses, a giving of the BEST, giving it as the FIRST PART and as seed for God to use and bless back to them.

Firstfruits giving is a living part of the system God has chosen for us in order to give His best back to us for our needs to be supplied . . . while we are still on earth.

God's Financial System is not for His prosperity, it is for our prosperity. *It is to bless us, that we may be a blessing.* It's that simple and important!

I remember when my brother Vaden and I gathered our corn harvest. When we pulled the ripe ears from the stalks and brought them into the barn, Papa would say, "Now, boys, put the biggest and best ears in a pile by themselves, and the rest in another part of the barn." When we asked why, he replied, "We must not eat our seed corn. Those biggest, best ears are what we'll plant next year for the biggest, best harvest."

This is precisely why God wants us to give Him our best.

That's what He multiplies back. Your needs and mine are so great we can't afford to eat or use our best seed on ourselves, but we let God have it to grow into His best harvests for us.

God had said, "I know Abraham will command his children after him" (Genesis 18:19). God meant He could count on Abraham to take his understanding of Him and pass it on as a blessing to his descendants. Therefore, Moses and the children of Israel — the seed of Abraham — understood that giving tithes and offerings to God was to acknowledge Him as:

- **THE MOST HIGH GOD**
- **POSSESSOR OF HEAVEN AND EARTH**
- **DELIVERER FROM ALL THEIR ENEMIES**

because this was the heart of what God meant to them. It was a supreme act of their love and worship to give Him their tithes and offerings.

When God told Abraham, "I will multiply thy seed as the stars of heaven" (Genesis 22:17), He included multiplying his tithes and offerings. Tithing became the central seed in the creative and multiplying force of their overall faith in WHO GOD WAS and WHO THEY WERE as God's Chosen People, then and now.

When we come to the final book of the Old Testament, soon we will see, perhaps for our first time, how all-important God values our giving of tithes and offerings to bring us into the FLOOD STAGE of His blessings . . . and the rebuking of Satan in his efforts to devour our lives. But don't skip over the next pages. Read and study what God is leading me to say to you so you can properly prepare yourself for that greatest experience of all: when God through Jesus Christ, our Savior, puts you into FLOOD STAGE.

SUMMED UP

1. It is the purpose of your faith to make God your Source.

2. God as your Source is also your Financial System.

3. Learn the joy of GIVING/LIVING in connection with your worship of God.

4. God always has a due season for you to reap from your sowing.

5. God's Financial System is for your prosperity.

6. Prepare yourself for God to put you into FLOOD STAGE.

*   *   *

What does this chapter say to you? Write it down — NOW.

_____

_____

_____

_____

_____

_____

_____

_____

_____

CHAPTER SIX

THE FLOOD STAGE BLESSINGS ABRAHAM RECEIVED ARE STILL IN EFFECT FOR YOU

In thee shall all families of the earth be blessed.
—Genesis 12:3

THE BLESSING THAT GOD pronounced over Abraham *has never ceased. It is still in effect today.* His blessing and multiplying power is operating around the clock for every child of God. God specifically said that the giving of tithes and offerings causes Him to open the windows of heaven and put His children in FLOOD STAGE. And Jesus further stated that our giving is to be a SEED we sow of our FAITH. We SOW it, God will GROW it, and we will REAP it (Galatians 6:7; Matthew 17:20; II Corinthians 9:10).

In all my study of the Word of God I have come to realize that the only part connected with tithing which we should avoid is the part frustrated religious leaders of Israel (and later Christianity) added to it, and that is the so-called "debt" part, or the so-called "paying" of tithes and offerings.

GIVE NOT AS A DEBT YOU OWE BUT AS A SEED YOU SOW

God's people have always had their peaks of joyous giving of tithes and offerings, and their valleys where in their disobedience they were made to feel they "owed" their tithes and offerings to God.

I can find no place in Abraham's life where he gave tithes as a debt he owed, or in Moses' life, or in the lives of the prophets, or in Jesus' life, that tithing is a debt we owe. The bringing of the tithes and offerings was always the happiest day in Israel. They were worshiping God, who was greater than all the gods of earth, who was blessing and multiplying them both supernaturally and naturally, and who was delivering them from ALL their enemies. Through "giving tithes and offerings" they were giving more seed to be "multiplied exceedingly." It was an unbeatable combination as they lined their faith up with God's system, instead of man's system.

However, let me say that *if* the giving of tithes (in the Old Testament) was something they "owed" — something they had to "pay" — then let me also point out unequivocally that when Jesus went to the cross to redeem us back from the devil — and from the curse of the law — *He paid it all!* If indeed there was a debt, it was PAID IN FULL by our Savior (Galatians 3:13).

We can freely say, *"I give not as a debt I owe, but as a seed I sow."*

St. Paul describes it as "giving and receiving" (Philippians 4:15). Second Corinthians 9:10 states, "God who gives seed to the sower, also multiplies the seed sown and increases the fruits of your righteousness." Jesus emphatically stated,

> "Give, and it shall be given unto you;
>   good measure,
>   pressed down, and
>   shaken together,
>   and running over . . ." (Luke 6:38).

This is the overflow! Our giving which Jesus speaks of is based on the faith of Abraham as fully trusting God — and of God's *blessing* him that he might *make* him a *blessing*. We who have faith in Christ by knowing WHO HE IS, and therefore knowing WHO WE ARE, give as Abraham did and we

65

enter into SEED-FAITH. Then we are on that same Foundation Faith and God says He will bless US and make US a blessing!

That day when Abraham and his servants had won the victory and delivered Lot and the people from captivity, the king of Sodom offered the "spoils" to Abraham. And Abraham acted upon his faith in God, declaring, "I have lift up mine hand unto the Lord, the most high God, the possessor of heaven and earth, that I will not take from a thread even to a shoelatchet [string], and that I will not take any thing that is thine, lest thou shouldest say, I have made Abram rich" (Genesis 14:22,23).

DON'T EXPECT BLESSINGS FROM POLLUTED STREAMS

See this scene. It is like it happened yesterday. Watch Abraham as he looks over all the treasures lying before him, riches untold. See him look at the king of Sodom, then raise his hand and declare, "God my Source will make me rich, not you."

Abraham knew the king of Sodom was a poor source to him, that what he offered was not his to offer. To Abraham, God was Possessor of the earth and all that it contained, also of heaven and all it contained. He saw that the king of Sodom believed he possessed these things and by offering to give them to Abraham, he was seeking to get Abraham to put him above the Most High God and make him his source. And that kind of source is like a polluted stream.

This is exactly what people seek to do to you and me today. They want to appear as being the ones in control, or the possessors, expecting us to put our dependence in them. Then when something happens, like losing our job, our position, our business, our friends, our money, these people turn away from us. If we have made them our source we have neither them nor God left.

Don't miss the meaning of what Abraham did that so powerfully affects you and me, as believers, today. Abraham once again established . . .

GOD IS MY SOURCE!

In GIVING of himself and his men to deliver Lot, and the king of Sodom and his people, Abraham EXPECTED to RECEIVE (to be blessed) NOT from those he had helped, but from the Most High God, Possessor of heaven and earth, and Deliverer from all his enemies . . . AND the only One who would make him RICH. Rich in the way riches really count, spiritually, physically, financially.

Remember these Three Keys of the Miracle of Seed-Faith: *

(1) Abraham looked to God as his SOURCE.

(2) Abraham GAVE and he gave first as a seed
he planted.

(3) Abraham EXPECTED to receive his
riches — his full harvest — from God
alone, his Source of Total Supply.

In spite of the fact that Abraham's faith refused what a man, the king of Sodom, offered, he knew God would cause people to give to him. Jesus says in Luke 6:38 *men* are used as *instruments* to bring money and other things into our hands. "Give, and it shall be given unto you; good measure, pressed down, and shaken together, and running over, SHALL MEN GIVE INTO YOUR BOSOM."

Notice it again. Jesus said, "*Shall men* give into your bosom." Yet, I repeat, Abraham would not accept from this particular man, the king of Sodom, because he sensed the king was trying to be his source. God the Source had many

*Use coupon on page 171 to order your FREE copy of MIRACLE OF SEED-FAITH.

other people He would touch to give to His servant Abraham. Abraham did not know at that time who they were, but by faith he KNEW his Source System would not fail him in giving to him in a direct way, and also give to him through men. He was giving to God and making God his Source, knowing in his heart God would use whatever instrument was necessary to bless him. This knowing in his heart was the faith he had in God his Source.

More than once different ones have sent checks to this ministry who do not personally like me and told me so. Each time, however, they said they "felt led by God to give."

AN INTERESTING LETTER I RECEIVED

I once got a letter and a very nice check for this ministry from a man who wrote:

> *Dear Oral Roberts,*
>
> *Enclosed is a check which I want to give for your ministry.*
>
> *But don't think I'm sending it to you because I like you, because I don't like you. I wouldn't walk across the street to hear you preach.*
>
> *I'm sending it because that's what God told me to do, and I'm obeying God.*

Well, I didn't know exactly what to do with that check, because of the way the man felt about me. Then at the bottom I read this:

> *P.S. When you read this letter, you are going to want to send my check back. Don't do it, because God told me to send it. But, remember, it's not because I like you. I'm just obeying God.*

We did return a check to another man when we learned he

was trying to "buy" the blessings of God. We just couldn't wait to get that kind of money out of our hands. God is our Source and He knows exactly how to "multiply our seed sown," who to move upon to give to us, how we are to receive it from Him through that particular instrument, and to know our "due season" is to come.

God says when we give to Him, "men will give into our bosom." HE causes them to do it. In our giving we must be in an *attitude of receiving* at all times because God is continuously multiplying our seed-sowing so we can REAP (Galatians 6:7). When I answer my mail to someone who has given, I tell them to: EXPECT! EXPECT! EXPECT!

THE MULTIPLIED BLESSING OF GIVING "TITHES OF ALL"

Abraham got into the spirit of giving, because he *gave tithes of ALL*. He didn't limit himself by trying to figure it to the dollar, or to the hour, or to the day, or to a few of his talents. He opened up and let himself go all-out toward God in his GIVING/LIVING.

There's a powerful statement in Genesis 24:1 that tells what God did for Abraham when his time came to die: "And the Lord had blessed Abraham *in all things*." The point is that God blessed Abraham in the totality of his life, a continuous whole-person blessing. That doesn't mean Abraham did not have difficulties, problems, and needs — or his ups and downs. It means that he never stopped giving tithes of all, of serving and putting God first in his life. And it means when God added up Abraham's "average," it was a life of Seed-Faith and God's "average" back to him was an all-encompassing blessing that lasted to the last moment of his life on earth . . . and went on to life eternal.

Can you say, "I give tithes of all"? Will you be able to say when life on earth is over, "God has blessed me in everything"?

Do you even believe it is possible? "It's possible for people like Abraham," you say. But when you are believing God as the Source System, as Abraham did, God's Financial System works the same in you today. I don't mean that you try to be an Abraham, but you walk in the "steps of his faith" and learn to release your own faith to God on a steady basis. It didn't happen to Abraham by accident, and it won't be an accident when it happens to you. It will happen because you are working with God's system that never fails.

IMPROVE YOUR AVERAGE

A friend of mine who gives when he feels like it and doesn't give when he doesn't feel like it, said, "Oral, you know me pretty well. And you understand Seed-Faith giving. How do you think I'm doing?"

I smiled and said, "You need to improve your average."

You know, many people don't seem to understand that this earthly life is going to end for each of us. Our years, like Abraham's, are going to creep up on us. We are going to be dealing with God not only in the *now*, but in the hereafter. At that time we want the recording angel to say, "God blessed him . . . her . . . in everything."

Just as that meant everything to Abraham, it will mean everything to you and me. By giving our best now, joyously and faithfully, God will not disappoint us.

SUMMED UP

1. The blessing of Abraham has never ceased.
2. Give not as a debt you owe but as a seed you sow.
3. Refuse to trust any source but God.
4. God will give to you directly and also cause men to give to you.
5. Like Abraham, open yourself to go all-out toward God in your GIVING/LIVING.
6. Are you able to say, "I give tithes of all"?
7. When this life is over, will you be able to say, "God has blessed me in everything"?
8. Keep your average up.

* * *

What does this chapter say to you? Write it down.

_____

_____

_____

_____

_____

_____

_____

_____

CHAPTER SEVEN

YOU'RE ONE OF GOD'S CHOSEN PEOPLE, TOO!

*And I will make my covenant between me and
thee, and will multiply thee exceedingly.*
— Genesis 17:2

IT IS IN THE NATURE of Abraham's faith that we see the nature of our personal faith: that it is the *creative* power of God.

The nature of Abraham's faith was to believe that God is Most High God, Possessor of heaven and earth, Deliverer from all our enemies, and because of that, he saw WHO GOD IS and WHO HE WAS and he gave tithes of all. The nature of God was then revealed. God said, "I will make my covenant between me and thee, and will multiply thee exceedingly" (Genesis 17:2). And also, "I will bless thee and make thee a blessing" (Genesis 12:2).

First, God made His covenant with Abraham. This was an agreement that God accepted Abraham's faith and through that faith God would multiply him beyond all telling. The blessing that God gave to Abraham would be used by God to MAKE him a BLESSING to multitudes of future generations, including you and me as Christians. Above all, out of Abraham's seed would come a people who would believe God as Abraham did, and instead of ONE man of faith, there would be a WHOLE people of faith, the Chosen People of God.

Second, the nature of Abraham's faith was miracle-working faith. Faith that enabled him to go into a miraculous covenant with God, a faith that would cause God to do the impossible: give him and his barren wife, Sarah, a son in their old age — the son of promise, a type of the Lord Jesus Christ. Abraham's faith caused God to miraculously intervene in his life at every point of need. Because by our faith we are "in Christ" and are therefore Abraham's sons and daughters, our faith is also miracle-working faith today. Remember miracles come from God, and God acts on our faith as we release it to Him and as we expect miracles. The secret of life is in expecting miracles. That really excites me.

Third, Abraham believed God and what He told him. In Hebrews 11:6 we are told, "Without faith it is impossible to please him: for he that cometh to God must believe that he is, and that he is a rewarder of them that diligently seek him."

FAITH IS DOING AS WELL AS BELIEVING

People are always saying, "Why doesn't God bless me like He did people in Bible days?"

Well, that blessing is here 100 percent for you but it isn't going to come to you accidentally. Faith is BELIEVING and believing is DOING. For example, when Abraham came to God he did something — he believed WHO GOD IS. God didn't do Abraham's believing for him. He came to Abraham (and He comes to each of us too), and it was Abraham's decision to respond to Him rather than reject or ignore Him.

He could have said, "Oh, there's nothing to that stuff about there being a true God."

He could have *reacted* and cried, "God, why don't You bless me with a son? You have promised to bless me and my seed exceedingly. How can this be unless You open my wife's womb and restore power to me at my age so we can conceive a child together?"

As they grew older and older, until under natural conditions the conceiving of a child was impossible, Abraham could have rejected God and said, "I will never trust God again." Instead, he *responded* to God in faith, saying, "I believe You will give me a son from my wife Sarah. I believe You will bless my seed and multiply it exceedingly."

GOD GETS BLAMED FOR EVERY BAD THING

A young mother has been writing to me whose father was taken in death while she was a small child. Her mother was left with her and her little brother and sister to grow up without a father. Twenty years later she is still bitter. When she talks about God she ends up saying, "I made up my mind never to look to God again because He caused this tragedy to happen and took my dad away."

Now every time something bad happens to her or to members of her family, she cries, "God is doing it to us again. Why should I go on living? Being dead would be easier than having to cope with life."

She takes everything bad as a slap from God, as if He is punishing her personally . . . and as if there is no devil.

I wrote her back that through Adam's yielding to the devil's temptation and turning away from God, he pulled himself and his organic, or natural, descendants out of harmony with God, and without this harmony the world has been plunged into separation from God. It wasn't God's choice but man's.

God through the centuries has seen man blaming Him for every bad thing. Therefore, He says, "When you come to God you must believe that He is [WHO HE IS], and that He is a Rewarder [Deliverer] of them who diligently seek Him." Then He says, "Without faith it is impossible to please God."

Since it is impossible to please God without faith, God has given each of us a full measure of it (Romans 12:3). However, having faith is not enough. We must continually learn to release it to God in order to please Him.

This young woman and I have been corresponding for over a year now. Because of this tragedy in her life, it was hard for her to believe that God is a good God and is for us, not against us. Gradually she is seeing that because of man's believing the devil rather than God, a curse is over the earth, and death was permitted to come in. Because of the curse of sin, the earth produces weeds more naturally than good grain, and tragedy strikes more naturally than blessing.

BY FAITH I KNOW . . .

Death struck my family in February 1977, when my oldest daughter, Rebecca, and her husband died in a plane crash in a Kansas wheat field. We were numb with shock, grief-stricken not only over the death of our dear ones but over their three little children left. We could have cried out, "Why, God? Why did You cause this to happen to us?" From the natural that would have been the easiest thing to do.

On the way over to the home to tell the children their mommy and daddy were gone, and hurting until we thought we would die, I began to feel my faith rising inside me. Words formed by the Spirit of God in my heart and I spoke them by an act of my faith: "God knows something about this we don't know." Over and over I said it as Evelyn and I held hands and looked to God our Source. Saying this vital truth permeated our beings. When we reached the children and told them their mommy and daddy were with Jesus and we and other close loved ones would take care of them in God's love, they knew in their little hearts that God did know something about it we did not know . . . and He would do what had to be done for them and us.

Things are working out and as much as I miss Rebecca and Marshall, even if I had the power, I wouldn't call them back. God is greater than death, and by faith I know it!

OUR FAITH MAKES THE DIFFERENCE

It's the same kind of world Abraham lived in. But it is our faith in God that makes all the difference. By his faith, Abraham refused to blame God for his wife's barrenness, or to blame her for a future, bleak, without a son, and for all the loneliness he faced as he believed God in the midst of bad people and bad things happening to him. By his faith he knew God was a good God and would reward his faith.

Jesus said, "The whole world lieth in wickedness" (I John 5:19). And He said, "[The devil] is the god of this world" (II Corinthians 4:4). Even Jesus, while in the flesh on earth, had to fight and struggle with the devil by using His faith the way Abraham did, and the same way you and I must do. Thank God we have faith and we can use it.

Fourth, Abraham exercised his will and believed God's promise of a son to him and Sarah, no matter what the obstacles. He believed God would multiply his seed because his worship of God and his giving tithes of all to God were in the same *rhythm of faith.* He was always planting seeds of faith: delivering his nephew Lot from captivity, feeding strangers who came his way, giving tithes of all, and looking to God his Source to *bless* him and *make* him a *blessing.*

You say, "But that was Abraham." That's true, but St. Paul says we are to "walk in the steps of that faith of our father Abraham" (Romans 4:12). This is New Testament teaching!

Abraham's steps of faith meant he had to keep on walking in faith. Abraham never stopped believing God for a son. He refused to give up. Then one day — it seemed so slow in coming — he and Sarah were able to conceive a son, and nine months later Isaac was born. It was a natural conception and birth, yet a faith miracle had caused it to happen. Abraham's faith had created the miracle-power to cause it to happen, just like your faith and mine has miracle-working power today to cause things to happen both naturally and supernaturally.

Isaac's birth was the beginning of the people who would come to be known throughout the world as "God's Chosen People." People who, as descendants of Abraham, responded to the faith he had taught his son Isaac. A people who came to believe that God was the Most High God, Possessor of heaven and earth, Deliverer from all their enemies, and Multiplier of their tithes given to Him for His cause, and to meet their needs.

Isaac begat Jacob, whose name was later changed to "Israel." And from Israel, came the twelve sons whose descendants were known as "the twelve tribes of Israel." Out of this people and nation came David and the household of David. And it was from David that our Savior, Jesus Christ, came, whom St. Paul calls the "seed of David" (Romans 1:3).

Notice that it was the seed of Abraham blessed and MULTIPLIED — THE SEED-FAITH PRINCIPLE — that brought forth both Israel and our Savior Jesus into the world.

A FAITH PEOPLE ESTABLISHED

Isaac, the seed of Abraham by a miracle of the supernatural acting on the natural, was the beginning of the nation of Israel, a faith people whom God established. They were chosen by God, and lived in the knowledge of God as Most High God, Possessor of all, Deliverer from all their enemies and the One to whom they gave "tithes and offerings." Although the rest of the world resented and hated them, it was still acknowledged that they were a delightful people — "a most delightsome land" (Malachi 3:12).

As these people of God obeyed the Lord, having the faith of Abraham to believe God as he did, and to give Seed-Faith tithes as he did, God's righteousness covered them the same as it had covered Abraham. When God looked at them He didn't see their faults or their shortcomings. He saw them clothed and covered in His own righteousness, for that is what their faith reflected.

What person is there, who deep down inside his soul does not want to stand righteous — in right relationship — before God? Isn't it our greatest desire to be at peace and in harmony with the Lord who is the Source of our lives? Isn't the struggle and turmoil which threatens the world, and our own lives, the result of men who care nothing about being joined to and covered by God and His righteousness?

You and I can learn something important from God's dealings with Abraham and the nation of Israel by remembering these important things in their relationships:

(1) Israel descended from Abraham and became a nation, not only in the physical sense, but by living and flowing in the *FAITH* of their father Abraham, and understanding that: GOD IS THE MOST HIGH GOD, POSSESSOR OF HEAVEN AND EARTH, AND DELIVERER FROM ALL OUR ENEMIES.

(2) Israel learned to recognize God as the SOURCE OF THEIR TOTAL SUPPLY and out of this marvelous experience they worked with His system by joyously GIVING TITHES OF ALL THEY HAD.

(3) God's blessings were upon those in Israel who walked in faith EXACTLY AS THEY HAD BEEN UPON ABRAHAM. GOD *BLESSED* THEM AND THEN *MADE* THEM A *BLESSING* TO OTHERS.

Realize this is a true picture of what God's people were like when they were WALKING IN THE FAITH OF ABRAHAM. They were so prosperous, so blessed, so anointed of

God that in the face of all opposition, all struggles, they conquered everything before them and had good success.

As long as they looked to God as their Source System, and followed His Financial System, His Blessing System functioned in their lives and they could not be defeated. Also, in being BLESSED, God MADE them a BLESSING. God multiplied their seed exceedingly, as He had promised Abraham. God always keeps His Word when we believe it and act by faith upon it.

YET ISRAEL LOST OUT WITH GOD

It is very important that you understand that these people who became God's Chosen People, when they stopped living by the faith of Abraham, lost out with God. Without God as their Source, they tried to go it alone. As sure as night follows day, they lost the blessings of God. Instead of being in FLOOD STAGE, they became captives to people who didn't even believe in God. They became a defeated people.

In the next chapter I want you to see their fatal mistake in TURNING AWAY FROM GOD and damming up their blessings, a mistake you can avoid.

SUMMED UP

1. Your faith is your creative power.
2. Make a faith covenant with God.
3. Faith is believing . . . therefore faith is something you do.
4. Stop blaming God for bad things happening to you. God is a good God, and He is always a good God.
5. Get into the rhythm of faith.
6. You are part of God's chosen people — a faith people.
7. By your faith God's righteousness covers your life.

What does this chapter say to you? Write it down.

_____

_____

_____

_____

_____

_____

_____

_____

_____

_____

_____

_____

_____

_____

_____

_____

_____

_____

CHAPTER EIGHT

A JOURNEY OF FAITH AND MIRACLES THAT VITALLY AFFECTS YOU TODAY

I will put none of these diseases upon thee, which
I have brought upon the Egyptians: for I am the
Lord that healeth thee. — Exodus 15:26

THE DESCENDANTS OF ABRAHAM, the children of Israel, God's chosen people, became the most victorious and successful people in the world! Their spiritual power, their physical health, their financial success, their faithfulness in teaching their children about God and His system, made them "a light to the nations." But they made a fatal mistake, and you must understand what this mistake was.

There came a time when they began turning from their faith that God was the Most High God. As individuals and as a people, they stopped believing that God owned heaven and earth: the natural and supernatural. *At that moment their faith ceased to be a miracle-working faith.* Without believing WHO GOD WAS and that He could deliver them from all their enemies, they no longer knew WHO THEY WERE. Hear it good, my friend, the people of Israel when they no longer knew WHO GOD WAS, forgot WHO THEY WERE.

You say, "What difference did this make?" Well, it was right here at this point where they lost their personal identity with the God of Abraham. They dammed up their Source. They STOPPED giving their tithes and offerings to God — which was the seed God would use to bless and multiply His work, and then bless and multiply it back to them to meet their own needs, OVER AND ABOVE, and get them into FLOOD STAGE. And that made all the difference in the world to what happened to them.

THE FATAL MISTAKE OF TURNING AWAY FROM GOD

They turned to other gods. And their number-one sin was idol worship — worshiping something other than God, perverting their God-instilled desire to worship Someone higher than themselves. Like millions today, they put these other gods before the Most High God and thought of Him only as a god of lower rank, if they thought of Him at all.

This is why they stopped *"giving tithes of all."* They had stopped trusting God as their Source of spiritual, physical, and financial supply. They clogged up the flow. Their thought was: why should we give tithes of all? They were cut off as surely as an unplanted field grows weeds when seed is not planted in it to grow a harvest. So without their continuous giving to God as Source of all, they LOST the One who would multiply their seed sown, cover them with His righteousness and deliver them from all their enemies.

The enemies they had easily defeated before were now able to defeat them, their victories turned into defeat, their supply turned into terrible lack and need.

They had been a people of joy and singing, a people of giving and receiving, and a people *blessed* and *made* a *blessing.* Now they had left the Most High God. They no longer released their faith. They tried to make it WITHOUT faith and utterly failed. Can you see yourself here at all? Can you see that you cannot make it on your own? Can you see that without God as your Source you will never be truly *blessed* and *made* a *blessing?*

DELIVERED FROM BONDAGE

In Moses' time when these same children of Israel had become captives in Egypt, God did not give up on them. He remembered the faith of His servant Abraham. He remembered how Abraham had "commanded" his descendants after him to live by faith. He remembered that faith was still in them, although lying dormant. And like a mother still loving her wayward children, God did not forget them. Oh, I love God for this. It means so much for us to know today that God does not forget us for all the times we become captives to somebody or some thing. He knows there is faith lying dormant in us ready to spring forth when we return to Him.

I remember when I left home as a young man, I left against my parents' wishes, wanting them and their talking to me about God to get out of my life. I little knew that every night I was away during those months Mamma would get out of bed after midnight and pray, "God, bring Oral home. Bring him home at any cost."

I remember how on the day I was leaving she pulled my long, lanky frame down to her five-foot height and kissed me, as her tears wet my face. Her words rang in my heart: "Oral, your father and I have taught you the way of the Lord. You will never get away from our prayers."

At that time I had no idea that I, like all others, had been created to look to God as my Source, to know that God was a good God, a God of blessing. I did not know Mamma was only feeling and saying what God felt about me, and that her caring for me was God caring.

GOD'S LOVE IS A CONTINUING LOVE

One of the evidences of God's continuing love for the children of Israel was what He did for them while they were in

Egypt, one of the most disease-ridden places on earth. He did NOT allow the diseases of Egypt to come on them! Although they were forced to be slaves, and were ultimately denied anything fit to eat, or work fit to do — being reduced to the absolute bottom — THERE WAS NO SICKNESS AMONG THEM. God was their healing stream, the Source of their health and wholeness. This is the truth! Can you take it in?

When the Egyptians sent their midwives to deliver the Hebrew women at childbirth in order to kill the babies, they were so healthy they had their babies before the midwives could reach them (Exodus 1:19). Now that was something!

God said, "I will put none of the diseases of Egypt upon you," and not a disease of Egypt came upon them in that land.

A miracle was happening! Though surrounded by cruelty and poverty, no sickness of the Egyptians was able to touch the bodies of the people of Israel. And they began once again to believe God for WHO HE IS. Their faith began to rise. Recognizing the God of Abraham as their DELIVERER, the shout went up: "God of Abraham, Isaac, and Jacob, deliver us from our enemies!"

God heard their cry and raised up Moses to lead His people out of indescribable bondage. As God's instrument of deliverance, Moses believed and obeyed God and stood before Egypt's Pharaoh, commanding him in the name of Israel's God, "Let my people go!"

Pharaoh hardened his heart and refused time after time. Moses refused to give up but released his faith in the God of miracles. Abraham's God of deliverance sent miracle after miracle. Pharaoh tried everything but he could not stop these miracles. He was finally glad to let God's people go!

LIVING BY FAITH AGAIN

When the children of Israel left Egypt as Moses led them, it was because they had begun living by their faith again. As a result, the Most High God caused a continuous stream of miracles to flow into their lives again. These are not just words I am saying, they are facts.

They were able to cross the Red Sea on its dry bed after God rolled the waters back, yet when Pharaoh's army rushed in to stop them, the waters rolled over them and destroyed them. It was beyond the belief of the Egyptians, yet it was a clear distinction of how God blesses those who live by faith. Now get this:

In their struggle to travel across the desert and wilderness in their 40-year journey to the land of Abraham, as long as they looked to God as their Source . . .

> every *spiritual* need was met,
> every *emotional* need was met,
> every *physical* need was met,
> every *financial* need was met,
> every *food* and *clothing* need was met.

They were able finally to enter the Promised Land with the shout of a king!

When Moses' time with them was completed, they were not left leaderless. God had a successor, the young Joshua. Moses had trained Joshua in the faith of Abraham and to trust God as his Source System, Financial System, and Blessing System. Joshua accepted that training and prepared himself.

Then Joshua was told to meditate on God's Word day and night, to be obedient to His instructions from the Lord, and he would *prosper* and be given *good success* (Joshua 1:8). There wasn't a hint of negativeness as Joshua believed God and became the successor to Moses.

Many times I am asked who will succeed me in this ministry of taking God's healing power to this generation. I have always answered in three ways:

First, God has shown me that success without a successor is failure.

1981-82 Oral Roberts University student body, faculty, and staff
God has shown me in this ministry that success without a successor is failure. And He has promised me that as I raise up my students at ORU to hear His voice . . . and to go to the uttermost bounds of the earth for Him, they will do a greater work than I have done. And I haven't a doubt about it. (Note: City of Faith in background was under construction when this photo was taken. Opening date, November 1981.)

Second, it's my business to believe and obey God, to preach, teach, pray for the sick and train others, and God who began this ministry will have the one, or ones, ready, willing, and able to head up this ministry.

Third, God has promised me that as I raise up my students at ORU to hear His voice . . . and to go to the uttermost bounds of the earth for Him, they will do a greater work than I have done. By faith, I see a healing stream flowing out of the City of Faith, a beginning of the healing of the nations (Revelation 22:2). And I haven't a doubt of it. Staying in faith, and living by faith, is the key to a successful future.

CAPTIVE AGAIN

The children of Israel were so like us — so human, with their God-given power of choice. Joshua called them together and said, "Choose ye this day whom ye will serve" (Joshua 24:15). Can you believe it? Again they chose to STOP believing God as Most High God, Possessor of heaven and earth, Deliverer from all their enemies, and therefore STOPPED GIVING *tithes and offerings.*

As I study these people, it amazes me that when they stopped knowing WHO GOD WAS, they ceased knowing WHO THEY WERE, and each time, they no longer kept up the rhythm of giving and receiving. They changed their GIVING/LIVING to WITHHOLDING/DYING.

WITHHOLDING FROM GOD PREVENTS OUR MIRACLE HARVESTS

Today as I deal with thousands of people, both individually and as groups, I see the same pattern. They get stirred up to believe God and soon they begin to know Him as their Source of Total Supply. They began to joyously plant their *seeds* of faith, giving out of their *need*, giving their *best* and expecting God to give them His *best*. As they SOW the seed, God GROWS it, and they begin REAPING miracle harvests of blessings in every area of their lives.

Then they get involved with man's system and forget God as their Source System, their Financial System, and their Blessing System. Soon they begin to break their giving rhythm. It doesn't seem to bother them until they run into real problems again. Then they start saying, "Why doesn't God help me?" forgetting that they have been robbing God and shutting Him off as their Source. As they withhold their giving from God, they are preventing their own miracle harvests from growing, for without their seed-planting God has nothing to multiply back. It gives the devil a foothold in their lives again, as a void is created for him to enter, and it stops God's Blessing System.

You and I cannot afford to allow this void, or emptiness, to come into our lives, or stay in our lives, because God has placed in us the eternal desire to worship Him. And if we don't worship Him we will worship something or someone else.

I am absolutely certain that the last thing we do to create this void, this emptiness in us, is to stop "giving tithes of all" as Seed-Faith to God. He is our Source System and the only One who gives us a Financial System that works and a Blessing System that BLESSES us and MAKES us a BLESSING. I am not just saying words here. I believe 100 percent that this is what God is saying. God is our Source in every way and in every thing. I hope you believe this too.

ISRAEL BECAME A DEFEATED PEOPLE

Look what happened. Israel, without God as their Deliverer, was invaded by enemy armies which had been easy to defeat before. The Assyrians came and captured the ten northern tribes of Israel and they became so assimilated with this world system that they have not been found since!

Many a child of God, once serving God and blessed by Him, has become such a part of the world system that you cannot distinguish him as a child of God anymore. This is such a loss to God, and to the person who does it . . . because God can no longer BLESS him and MAKE him a BLESSING.

The two remaining tribes — Judah and Benjamin, who controlled Jerusalem and the southern kingdom — were invaded by King Nebuchadnezzar of Babylon. The walls of the city were torn down, the temple Solomon had built was destroyed, and the very flower of the nation — including the Hebrew young people — were taken into captivity in Babylon, a city which worshiped the golden idol which the king had made.

Some seventy years passed while they were in Babylonian captivity as the land of faithful Abraham lay in ruins, the city of Jerusalem in disrepair, the temple gone, their faith all but disappeared.

The prophets, such as Jeremiah, Ezekiel, Daniel, were calling on the people, "Return to God that He may bless you again."

Because of their stubborn refusal to live by the faith of God again, a spiritual blindness came over the people. Their spirits dried up. They no longer played their instruments or sang the songs of Zion or knew the blessing of the God of Abraham. (Read Psalm 137.)

The covenant God had made with Abraham because of his faith in WHO GOD WAS, WHO HE HIMSELF WAS, and therefore caused him to GIVE TITHES OF ALL, was broken. *God did not break His covenant with Israel.* They broke it. During those years of captivity in Babylon God's covenant continued, but without their faith it did not function in their lives.

THE ONLY WAY IS GOD'S WAY

Finally the prophet Nehemiah and the scribe Ezra stirred up the people to return to Jerusalem. These, with others like Malachi and Haggai, knew the only way was God's way.

A remnant came with Nehemiah to rebuild the walls of the city of God, building under the most terrible opposition and persecution. Then they set about to restore the temple and its services to the Lord. The God of Abraham honored their faith and hard work by blessing their efforts.

However, many who returned came on the faith of others instead of their own. Instead of helping build God's house again, they only built houses for themselves (Haggai 1:2-4). The idea of "giving tithes of all" that there might be resources in God's house and that He would again OPEN THE WIN-

DOWS OF HEAVEN to them was gone from their minds, because they no longer knew God as Most High God to them. By their own choice they had cut themselves off from walking in the faith that Abraham had in God.

For the final time, these people were about to cut themselves off from their Source. When the prophets Haggai and Malachi called on them to reconnect their lives with God, they had terrible needs, but by this time they did not connect the supplying of those needs with giving tithes of all to God, their Source System.

AND THIS IS EXACTLY what so many people who think of themselves as God's people are doing today. St. Paul says, "They have a form of godliness but deny the power thereof" (II Timothy 3:5). Notice, the power of God, which is both natural and supernatural, is no longer working God's wonders in their lives.

When water is cut off at its source, you cannot get water. And you cannot live without water.

The same is true of God. When you cut yourself off from Him, despite what you claim to be religiously, you will not know WHO GOD IS, nor will you know WHO YOU ARE, and you will stop your GIVING/LIVING.

This is what happened to most of the Chosen People of God after He enabled them to return to Jerusalem, where His house was restored and He waited to bless them. They were no longer in position to RECEIVE His spiritual, emotional, physical, and financial blessings.

Is it too late for you? No, it's not too late if you start acting on your faith now. In the next chapter you will see a good God opening the road back. This chapter is very important to you.

SUMMED UP

1. God has instilled in you a desire to worship Him.
2. In spite of everything, God has not forgotten you.
3. The moment you start living by faith again, God begins to bless you again.
4. You have the God-given power of choice . . . and you are choosing God or the devil.
5. God's Financial System will still work for you today.
6. You cannot live without God as your Source.
7. It's not too late if you start acting on your faith . . . now!

* * *

What does this chapter say to you? Write it down.

_____

_____

_____

_____

_____

_____

_____

_____

_____

CHAPTER NINE

MALACHI'S BURDEN FOR GOD'S PEOPLE TO GET INTO FLOOD STAGE IS MY BURDEN FOR YOU

The burden of the word of the Lord to Israel by Malachi. — Malachi 1:1

IT'S BEEN A LONG road since Abraham, since Moses, since Joshua, since the judges and kings of Israel, since the prophets. Through them God had taken the faith of ONE man, Abraham, and made it the faith to build a WHOLE people.

At last the remnant has returned from Babylon, not of the ten lost tribes of Israel, but of the two tribes, Judah and Benjamin, led by Nehemiah in rebuilding the walls and temple of Jerusalem, and by Ezra in restoring God's laws.

Other prophets — Zechariah, Haggai — have helped reconnect the people to the faith of Abraham, but now only ONE prophet is left. Time is about to run out on these people who descended from Abraham and who had known the blessing of Abraham but who have thrown that blessing away.

But God won't quit or give up on these people who once walked His paths. He stirs up the heart of a lone man of faith and a burden for them inspires him to write the final book of the Old Covenant (what we know as the Old Testament). If you were to pick up your Bible and turn to the last Old Testament book, you would see that it is written by the prophet Malachi who the people resented but who cared for them.

The book opens with Malachi's pouring out his heart. You must hear what he says because he is talking in the most personal way to you also: "The burden of the word of the Lord to Israel by Malachi."

I IDENTIFY WITH MALACHI

What I am writing today could be titled: "The burden of the word of the Lord's healing power to the people by Oral Roberts." For I too have a burden. I too care. The burden and the care of the Lord came on me in 1947 when — after a period of studying God's Word almost day and night, of intermittent fasting and prayer, of seeking after God with my whole being — God awakened me night after night with the same dream. In the dream God illumined my spirit and let me see people as He sees them, and hear them as He hears them. What I saw . . . and heard . . . almost took my breath away and marked me for life. I saw that everybody is sick in some way! Everybody has dis-ease! Everybody has needs and hurts of some kind!

Then I *heard* people as God hears them. In my spirit I heard everybody crying, either outwardly or inwardly, as they were being ripped apart by sin, sickness, fear, demons, poverty, and every other destructive force.

I have not looked on anyone since 1947 without knowing that that person is sick in some way — spiritually, emotionally, physically, or financially — and can come into health and wholeness only as he knows God as his Source and follows His system by faith.

I know God *sees* and *hears* people like this because it is the way He lets me *see* and *hear* them. And this *seeing* and *hearing* them that I have in my spirit has never gone away. It stirs me, tears at me, and drives me with a compassion that is with me day and night.

Years ago I found this poem and wrote it down on the flyleaf of my Bible. Under it I wrote, "This is the way I feel toward the sick." It's been that way since 1947, and it will be with me the rest of my life.

The Shepherd

Where are you going, shepherd?
> To find my sheep.

How far will you go?
> As far as my sheep.

How far may that be?
> To the world's end.

How long will you seek it?
> Until I find it.

When you find it, will it come to you?
> No, it will flee from me.

Where will it go then?
> To the rocks and the sand.

When will it stop?
> When it can run no more.

What will you do then?
> Carry it home.

I know this is how Jesus, the Good Shepherd, feels toward the sick for He has put that same feeling in me. And it is one of the things that stands out to me in the physicians I know who are the most effective. They have an acute sensitivity to sick people and a deep compassionate desire to get them well. Jesus said, "They that are sick need a physician" (Luke 5:31), and every one of us does. One of St. Paul's most effective co-laborers was a physician whom he called, "Luke, the beloved physician" (Colossians 4:14).

When God inspired men to write the books of the New Testament, He chose Dr. Luke to write the Gospel of Luke, to show more of the human side of Jesus as He ministered to the

I have not looked on anyone since 1947 without knowing that that person is sick in some way — spiritually, emotionally, physically, or financially — and can only come into health and wholeness as he knows God as his Source and follows His system by faith.

people; and also to write the Book of Acts, to show both the NATURAL AND SUPERNATURAL power of God at work in the first Christians as they preached, taught, and healed . . . working with God's system and blazing a trail of miracles for us to follow today.

I have known through all the years of this ministry the "burden of the Lord" He put in me to take His healing power to this generation, and to merge His healing streams of medicine and prayer, putting the natural and supernatural together where they belong. When Malachi wrote, "The burden of the Lord by Malachi," I can identify with him. The burden for the people originates in God, but the Lord transfers it to us and it becomes the motivating force to take God's delivering power to hurting people.

BUILDING THE CITY OF FAITH

In building the vast *City of Faith Medical and Research Center* on the ORU campus here in Tulsa, the largest medical center under one roof in the world, and the first of its kind in history, built to minister to over one million sick people a year, the burden of the Lord has nearly consumed me.

In addition to carrying on this full-time ministry of preaching, teaching, and healing . . .

- of conducting the affairs of the Oral Roberts University, with its thousands of students whom I am to raise up to "hear God's voice and to go where His voice is heard small, His light is seen dim, His power is not known, and to go to the uttermost bounds of the earth,"
- of continuing to innovate new ways and methods of using television, including prime time, and at the same time helping my son Richard develop his own ministry of the Lord's healing power,
- of publishing our two magazines (ABUNDANT LIFE and DAILY BLESSING), writing two books a year, of answering the letters from hurting people who write me so I can pray for them more personally,
- of being a part of my beloved home city, Tulsa, and the work of the Lord through His church here and world-wide,
- of being a man, a husband, father, and grandfather . . .

I have felt at times I literally could not carry this burden. The misunderstanding and deliberate persecution which has come along with it has struck like a knife in my back.

I am saying all these things to make a much more important point. The point is that the burden of the Lord for people exists. It's real, and has been ever since the first man went away from God. God cares and keeps on caring.

But God has to have men and women to share this burden. Malachi put it like this: *The burden of the word of the Lord by Malachi.* Not simply the Lord's burden, but Malachi's too.

Sometimes I try to explain that while God has said to "cast all your cares on him" (I Peter 5:7), He never takes back a burden He puts on one of His servants to carry His Word and power to the people (Romans 11:29).

I am sure the news media of Malachi's day ripped him. Certainly the people he tried to deliver did. But he could bear it, the same way I can and you can, because the Lord's burden by him, if heeded, would deliver the people and bring them into the FLOOD STAGE of the Lord's blessings — spiritually, emotionally, physically, and financially. It would restore them to God as their . . .

Source System,
Financial System, and
Blessing System.

When I refer to my part of the Lord's burden for the people, two things stand out to me:

>**One,** I have, by my determination to obey God and His constant anointing upon me, been able to stay well and carry on this ministry without stopping once since 1947. Today I am in beautiful health.

>**Two,** the enemies of this ministry have misrepresented, hindered, and done all they can to put it in a bad light, but God just keeps on shining His light on it, and more and more people continue to receive help.

To know the devil throws his biggest weapons and still the ministry goes forward, is the glory of our God round about us.

The vast City of Faith Medical and Research Center is a 20-story research center, 60-story clinic, and 30-story hospital where we are combining God's healing streams of prayer and medicine. It is the largest medical center under one roof and on one base in the world, and the first of its kind in history. At full operation the City of Faith will minister to over one million sick people a year. (Photo taken just before opening.)

In the hospital part of the City of Faith, each two floors are joined by an atrium, with a Prayer Tower replica as the focal point. This expanse of space eliminates the closed-in feeling of long narrow halls and the usual hospital atmosphere. We believe this is a vital part of the healing process.

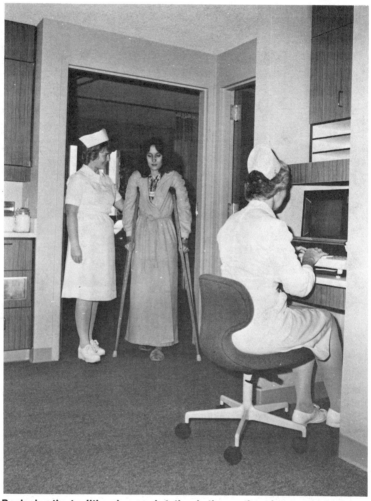

Replacing the traditional nurses' station is the nursing alcove, which places the nurse and the prayer partner only a few steps from the patient's bedside.

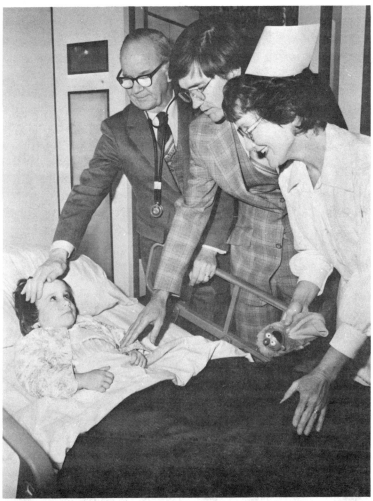

A physician, prayer partner, and nurse minister to a pediatric patient in the City of Faith.

The Healing Hands in front of the City of Faith, the largest cast bronze sculpture in the world, represent the hand of medicine and the hand of prayer joined together for the healing of humanity. (The Grand Atrium in the background, a 13-story visitors center, was unfinished when this photo was taken.)

GOD HAS TO STOP US SOMETIMES TO GET US STARTED

My darling wife Evelyn just came in where I am writing and handed me a letter. The last two paragraphs say:

> *I want you to use my Seed-Faith gift for the City of Faith. I am glad you followed God's message and built the City of Faith in order to send His Word and healing power to the ends of the earth. I have prayed for your work and believe that nothing can stop it, as long as God is served and people are helped. What you do may be turned down by some men, but when God ordered it, He also gave you the power to accomplish His goals. You could never have "thought up" all you have done, and are doing. It had to be God. I rejoice and thank God with you for it all.*

> *Bless Richard and Evelyn for sharing your responsibility and helping you. I know it seems like a long time since you nearly lost your life to tuberculosis and you lay on the gym floor hemorrhaging, but God has to stop us sometimes just to get us started.*

I remember that gymnasium floor in the final game of a district basketball tournament. I, too, had left God and desperately needed to return to Him. To know that I returned to God in the midst of my dying and began living anew means hope to you . . . and is proof that if God can use a flawed person like Oral Roberts, He can use anybody!

SUMMED UP

1. God doesn't give up on His people . . . including me.
2. God's prophet, Malachi, the last of the prophets before Jesus came, carried the burden of the Lord for His people.
3. God cares enough for me that He sends His servants to help me return to Him.
4. The City of Faith Medical and Research Center combining God's healing streams is a new hope for my health and wholeness.
5. Today I can begin living anew.

* * *

Write down what this chapter said to you — right now.

_____

_____

_____

_____

_____

_____

_____

_____

_____

_____

CHAPTER TEN

GOD DEALS WITH YOU IN LOVE

I have loved you, saith the Lord. — Malachi 1:2

IT TAKES A LOT of love to tell someone the truth. Truth isn't always easy to take. The children of Israel had been robbing God. It had not been thought possible that those who descended from the faith of Abraham would ever rob God, but it happened on such a scale that the windows of heaven had been shut up against them financially.

From the beginning of God's Financial System, instituted in the faith of Abraham for His people of all time, God's people had been prospered and blessed through it. God had rebuked their enemies, made their crops grow, and put the money in their hand for His work, and for all their own financial needs. They were a financially blessed people, because God's Financial System never fails.

Now because they had first broken God's Spiritual System, they also broke God's Financial System by robbing Him. It is bad to rob any of God's creatures but to rob God — that is unthinkable.

God knew He had been robbed . . . by the people He loved and had blessed. In the rebuilding of Solomon's Temple, destroyed 70 years before, the worship services were barely being carried on. The spiritual leaders were not receiving the tithes (tenth) of the people because they were withholding them for their own private use. *Seedtime and harvest* had virtually stopped for the first time since Noah. The tithes of all, as given by Abraham, had been totally withheld from the Most High God for the first time since Abraham. The "firstfruits" of the land had not been brought by the people and given to the Lord. The giving of the tithe of their money had stopped. God's house, the place where God met His people in those days, was almost empty and God said, "There is no meat [resources] in my house."

GOD DID NOT CHANGE; HIS PEOPLE CHANGED

God had said, "The tithe is the Lord's." God had said, "The offerings are mine." Both tithes and offerings belonged to God but were being withheld by the people and used for themselves.

God knew He had been robbed because the power He had used to multiply the seed of His people was now dormant. Because they were not giving, there was no seed for God to "multiply exceedingly." They had literally stopped God from blessing them financially and because of that, they missed other blessings too.

If you had your money in a bank and the banker was paying regular interest to you, and you withdrew your money, the banker would know it if for no other reason than that the bank's interest payments had stopped. He would know by the stopping of the interest payments that your money had been withdrawn.

When God's power "to get wealth" is not being poured out on His people, *He* knows something is wrong! When we think of our financial lack, *we* know something is wrong. We know we are not working with God's Financial System.

IN ROBBING GOD, WE ROB OURSELVES

The question was how to break the news to those God loved when they had robbed Him, and had continued robbing Him until God saw them no longer as His Chosen People but as robbers and thieves. He knew that in robbing Him, they were actually robbing themselves. They were cutting themselves off from God as their Source System, their Financial System, and their Blessing System.

The people of God! The apple of His eye. Robbers? Yes! The heirs of Abraham's faith, robbers? Yes! The ones who had heaven and earth — both the natural and supernatural opened to them — were robbers? Yes!

When God said, "You have robbed me," they scornfully asked, "Wherein have we robbed thee?" God answered, "In tithes and offerings."

In their hearts they were saying, "God, You mean by our not giving tithes and offerings, that is robbing You? How could just a tenth of what we possess not being given affect You so much? How could that make us robbers?"

God said, "You should consider how it affects you! A curse is now on your blessings. You have rejected Me so completely as Most High God, Possessor of heaven and earth, and Deliverer from all your enemies, that your unbelief and ingratitude has blinded you. By withholding your tithes and offerings, you are stealing from the God of your father, Abraham."

WILL A MAN ROB GOD?

Then God asked the question that rings through the centuries, a question not only to the Hebrew people, not only to the Christian people, but to the whole human species: "Will a man rob God?"

Has man, who was made in the image and likeness of his Creator, forgotten his own divinity and humanity so much that he steals from his own life Source?

LUCIFER, THE ARCHANGEL, ROBBED GOD

God is referring back to the great archangel Lucifer, who had robbed Him. Yes, Lucifer the most beautiful of all the angels, the one God had placed over the silver and gold of the earth and all the precious gems, the one who was nearest the throne. He had robbed God by saying, "I will ascend into heaven, I will exalt my throne above the stars of God: I will sit also upon the mount of the congregation, in the sides of the north: I will ascend above the heights of the clouds; I will be like the most High" (Isaiah 14:13,14).

Lucifer also knew God as *Most High God.*

When God saw that Lucifer had wrongfully exercised his power of choice — irrevocably changing his nature from *"torch bearer"* to darkness itself, becoming a robber of God and of His creation — God acted swiftly and cast him down to earth. Christ was present in heaven and saw this awesome scene. Later in His earthly ministry, through which He had come to destroy the works of the devil, Jesus recalled, "I beheld Satan [the former Lucifer] as lightning fall from heaven" (Luke 10:18).

God knew Lucifer had robbed Him and, becoming the devil, had been cast out of heaven. Now He asks, "Will a M-A-N rob God?"

To Lucifer, God had said, "You have sinned," and heaven was closed to him forever. He was put under a curse and *reserved in the chains of darkness* (Jude, verse 6). The darkness, or lack of spiritual illumination, understanding, and obedience, became the *chains* of Lucifer and the other angels that fell with him. As the "god of this world" (II Corinthians 4:4), and the "prince of the power of the air" (Ephesians 2:2), Satan's purpose has been to steal man away from God, and to get man to rob God as he himself had done.

Now God's question is, "Will a *man* rob God?"

Before you can answer, you have to understand the question. Will you, who are not an angel but a human being, a creature made lower than the angels (Psalm 8:5; Hebrews 2:7), rob God? Will *you* steal from God?

In other words, God is asking, "Will you be like the devil,

who Jesus described as the one coming only to steal, to kill, and to destroy" (John 10:10).

God's question, "Will a man rob God?" goes all the way back to Lucifer's robbing God, which made him the devil.

When God asks you, "Will you as a human being rob God?" He is putting you on alert that you have two ways to go with the love He has for you:

One, to worship God, your Creator and Redeemer, to know WHO HE IS and then know WHO YOU ARE, and give "tithes of all" as Seed-Faith so He can BLESS you and MAKE you a BLESSING, or

Two, to choose to set in motion those negative forces that will cause the windows of heaven — the supernatural and natural — to be closed up against you. With the windows of heaven closed, a curse will be on your blessings, and this world system will be a poor substitute compared to the Most High God being your Source System, your Financial System, your Blessing System.

My friend, again read these two ways you are choosing to go. Re-read them carefully and examine your heart before God.

WHAT ROBBING GOD HAS DONE

I want you to look around you and see how men have allowed the devil to take over. God said through the prophet Haggai, "The silver is mine, and the gold is mine, saith the Lord of hosts."

Are the silver and gold in the hands of the righteous? Are the tithes of all the silver and gold — and what they control — being given to God because of WHO HE IS?

When you read of people buying up and hoarding most of the silver, do you think they are doing it for God? Or gold — it is fought over by the speculators until they bid it up so high it throws the economics of entire nations into inflation and unemployment. Do you think that is being done for the glory of God? Do you think the holders of the gold are giving "tithes of all" to God?

Do you see what robbing God has done? Even when the people who do not acknowledge God have most of the money and we as God's people do not, we have developed the attitude, "Well, poor little ole me. I'm not supposed to have anything on this earth, but I'll have it all in heaven."

Listen, friend, you may live a long time before you go to heaven, every minute of which you will live on THIS earth! It is here you need God's Financial System working 100 percent for you. You won't need money in heaven.

How can we read St. Paul's mighty words in Philippians 4:19, "My God shall supply all your need according to His riches in glory by Christ Jesus," and not get our faith stirred up to believe God to supply our everyday earthly needs according to all of God's riches both in heaven and on earth?

IT'S DIFFICULT TO SEE OURSELVES

At a recent Oral Roberts University Seminar I spoke on this very subject. Afterwards I asked a young man in the audience what he had learned from my message.

"I learned that I have not been giving," he responded.

"Does that mean you have been robbing and stealing from God?" I asked.

He shuffled his feet and hesitated a little, then answered, "It means I just haven't been giving."

Then I pointed out Malachi 3:8 which says if we've stopped giving, we are actually stealing and robbing from God.

I asked the young man again, "Have you been stealing from God by withholding your tithes and offerings?"

He said, "I prefer the word 'taking'."

To make my point, I said, "But the Bible says 'stealing' and 'robbing'."

Finally he said, "I am going to be honest with God. Yes, I've been robbing God, and because of stealing from Him I have been robbing myself!"

To say the actual words *stealing* and *robbing* was hard for him to do. Aren't we all like that young man? Each of us finds it difficult to admit, even to ourselves, that we are robbing and stealing from God, and because of it we are taking away God's blessings from ourselves.

I finally asked this young man if he felt better after making his confession. He said, "It's like a heavy load is lifted. I feel good because I now know what to do to put things right between me and God."

How can we, as children of God, rob God in tithes and offerings — as seed for Him to use and multiply — or go one more hour without giving God our best, yet expect Him to give us His best?

How can we continue to blame God for the *bad things* happening to us financially, if we are breaking God's Financial System? Remember, when you deal with money, and the tithes and offerings of it, you are dealing with God himself — the Most High God, Possessor of heaven and earth, Deliverer from all your enemies, Multiplier of your seed sown. In your giving you are dealing with the Name of Jesus, which God has exalted and made above everything that is named in this world and the world to come (Ephesians 1:20,21).

St. Paul said in Galatians 6:7: "Be not deceived; God is not mocked: for whatsoever a man soweth, that shall he also reap."

First, Paul says, "Don't be deceived." Don't deceive yourself into thinking you can gain by robbing God. If Lucifer, the highest archangel, couldn't gain by it, neither can you . . . and don't make yourself believe you can.

Second, Paul says, "God is not mocked." People can act like they are mocking God by believing they can sow one thing and reap another, but there is no way they can mock God by changing His system of Seedtime and Harvest. God made His system for our good and no power will ever change it.

Third, Paul says, "Whatsoever a man sows, that shall he also reap." WHATSOEVER he sows, THAT (and that alone) will he REAP!

That! That! That!

THE MAN WHO GAVE WITH A TEASPOON

I once heard a story about a man who gave to the Lord with a teaspoon. He always gave the smallest amounts possible. There was no joy in his giving, so he gave the least he could to salve his conscience. One day he had a desperate need and asked God to give to him.

God said, "Give Me your teaspoon."

"Lord, that isn't big enough," the man said. "I need You to use a shovel!"

The Lord answered, "Then give with a shovel."

This means we are to give God our biggest and best so we can ask Him to give us His biggest and best.

The children of Israel had robbed God until the very seed they planted had a curse on it. It was totally polluted. And *that* is what they reaped — the produce from cursed AND polluted (poisoned) seed.

I've heard Christians say, "No matter what I do, nothing works out for me." The first thing that comes to my mind is Malachi's words: *your seed is cursed and polluted.* The next thing I think is that *you've been giving with a teaspoon.* Because if you and I sow GOOD seed, giving out of our NEED, giving our BEST, and giving FIRST, God says, THAT is what we REAP! It is as St. Paul says in II Corinthians 9:6,7: "But this I say, he which soweth sparingly shall reap also sparingly; and he which soweth bountifully shall reap also bountifully. Every man . . . as he purposeth in his heart, so let him give;

not grudgingly, or of necessity: for God loveth a cheerful giver."

This is the truth God tells us about ourselves, but because He loves us He doesn't leave us where we are. He offers His system to us because He is the SYSTEM. But He also sets conditions for the blessings of His system to come into FLOOD STAGE for us. We put the system into motion.

SUMMED UP

1. God tells me the truth because He loves me.
2. When I break God's Spiritual System, I also break His Financial System.
3. My tithes and offerings are the Lord's — my Seed-Faith to Him to multiply exceedingly to bless me.
4. Lucifer was the first to rob God and he became the devil. When I rob God I am being like the devil who wants it all for himself.
5. I must use my God-given power of choice to choose to give to God or to withhold and rob Him — and myself.
6. I need God's financial supply in FLOOD STAGE while on this earth. I won't need it in heaven.
7. I will stop blaming God for bad things happening to me financially, and check myself to see if I am robbing Him.
8. Whatever I sow, that is what I will reap; therefore, I will sow my best seeds to God.
9. I must understand God's Financial System to get into FLOOD STAGE.

What does this chapter say to you? Write it down.

_____

_____

_____

_____

_____

_____

_____

_____

_____

_____

_____

_____

_____

_____

_____

_____

CHAPTER ELEVEN

"RETURN UNTO ME" — GOD SETS THE CONDITIONS FOR HIS FLOOD STAGE BLESSINGS TO COME TO YOU

Return unto me, and I will return unto you, saith the Lord of hosts. — Malachi 3:7

EVERYTHING GOD DOES is in love. But you set His love in motion by your response to Him. Malachi is burdened and delivers God's words to the people: "I have loved you, saith the Lord" (Malachi 1:2).

In the New Testament St. John tells us, "God is love" (I John 4:8). But he is only restating an eternal truth. God has always loved because love is His nature.

When you think of how often you and I have failed to obey God, and still God keeps on loving us, we can't help but fall on our knees crying, "God, I am not worthy. But thank You for loving me."

God was telling His people again, "I have loved you."

Yet they ask, "Wherein have you loved us?" (Malachi 1:2).

How could God count the ways? He loved them when He came to them in their bitter bondage in Egypt and brought them out with a high hand to the land of their father Abraham. They had come out of Abraham's faith and by taking hold of that faith, God had given them the blessing of Abraham: "Surely blessing I will bless thee, and multiplying I will multiply thee." And, of course, this is the greatest blessing any person or any people can ever have.

God had let His people look above the gods of men and see Him who is . . .

> Most High God,
> Possessor of heaven and earth,
> Deliverer from all our enemies,
> Multiplier of all our tithes and offerings.

They had seen Him as their Source, and knew they would have lack for nothing.

They had seen their deliverance come from all their enemies — spiritually, emotionally, physically, and financially.

God had blessed them. He had made them the head and not the tail, placed them above and not beneath, given them power to get wealth, put none of the diseases of Egypt on them, looked at them through His own righteousness, and told them they were the apple of His eye.

GOD PUT WINNING IN HIS PEOPLE BUT THEY THREW IT AWAY

Malachi tells them that God calls them to task because of their disobedience — their repudiation of all that was good for them by their refusal to walk in the faith of Abraham, the Foundation Faith for all people.

God said to them:

> *If ye will not hear, and if ye will not lay it to heart, to give glory unto my name, saith the Lord of hosts, I will even send a curse upon you, and I will curse your blessings . . . because ye do not lay it to heart. Behold, I will corrupt your seed, and spread dung upon your faces, even the dung of your solemn feasts; and one shall take you away with it* (Malachi 2:2,3).

These words seem harsh, but life is real and God was concerned for His people because THEY had cut THEMSELVES off from faith, from love — from Him their only Source. He was concerned — and angry — at what they were doing to themselves.

Poisonous weeds were growing instead of the pure seed they were to have planted for miracle harvests in a world which didn't believe in miracles. Their enemies were winners instead of them. God had put the winning in His people but they had thrown it away. Their needs were overwhelming them although He was the Source to meet all their needs. Disease was destroying their health even though He had said, "I am the Lord that healeth thee." Can you not see in this that God is a good God, and is always a good God?

YOU CAN GET THE CURSE OFF YOUR BLESSINGS

Cursed blessings and polluted seed — these are not what God wants us to have. We are told by St. Paul in Galatians 3:13,14 that Jesus fulfilled the Old Covenant by giving us a new and better one, "being made a curse for us."

Jesus took the curse, He took the pollution, He took our stealing from God and ourselves and bore them on the cross so we are FREE from them — *if we choose to be.*

Jesus has already done His part. He isn't going to the cross again. He isn't going to rise from the dead again. He has done it all for us!

Now, there doesn't have to be a curse on our blessings or a pollution of our seed. We can prove God for ourselves by giving all our tithes *and* offerings as good seed to Him to bless and multiply — which is the blessing of Abraham that is still in effect today.

"Return unto me," God says, "and I will return unto you" (Malachi 3:7). He is talking about WHO HE IS, not who this ungodly world system thinks He is. You see, God does not leave His people; they leave Him.

The Lord was saying:

"Return unto Me! Come back to Me! Leave the phony gods you are following. They are nothing.

"Turn away from thinking you control the heaven and the earth, the natural and supernatural. You don't!

"Turn away from trusting only in earthly powers to deliver you. They can't!

"Come back to me. I can deliver you from all your enemies!"

But when God said, "Return unto me," they didn't even know they had gone. You know, it's bad enough to leave God by failing to use your faith, but it's even worse not to know you are gone!

These people had not acknowledged receiving their blessings from God, who was their Source, but had taken those blessings from the earth and from heaven without a thankful heart. They had let man and earthly things become their source. Unlike Abraham, whose faith would not allow anyone but God to make him rich, they tried to get rich through man only.

THE SAD RESULTS

When God said, "Return unto me, and I will return unto you," they answered, "What do you mean, 'return unto me'?"

God answers them by asking a question, "Will a man [generic for man or woman] rob God? Yet ye have robbed me" (v. 8).

Then they ask, "Wherein have we robbed thee?"

God answered, "In tithes and offerings. As a result, your seed is corrupted (too poisonous to plant for a good harvest) and there is a curse on your blessings (you are miserable in spite of your possessions)."

I deal with many people who at one time loved God, loved the church, loved giving tithes and offerings and planting them as their *seeds of faith*. They loved to read and study the Bible, to hear it preached and taught. They loved to call on God, they wanted to feel His presence, to know Him in their hearts in a personal way, to have a close walk with Him. Yet today, even as members of churches, they are some of the unhappiest, neediest people I know. Why is this?

In a real sense, they are either disappointed in God, or mad at God, or are ignoring Him in their daily lives. Many of them use God's name as a curse word. They use "four letter" words and don't even know how dirty their language is! They get mad at the government, rail at public officials, gripe about jobs or loss of jobs, get jealous of others who are living by faith — in short, they have no Source for their lives. Yet they want prayer like magic . . . one little prayer that will answer everything and put them in clover NO MATTER WHETHER THEY HAVE RETURNED TO GOD OR NOT!

Is this you? Or does it resemble you in any way?

GOD SETS THE CONDITIONS

Recently some men came to get me to pray for a certain high public official who was dying with an incurable disease. I was perfectly willing until they said, "Here are the conditions."

They began to lay out what I was to do. I said, "Can the man come for the preaching of God's Word first, since 'faith comes by hearing and hearing by the word of God' (Romans 10:17), then receive my prayers?"

"Oh, he's too busy. He's traveling and speaking and he doesn't have time for that."

"He has time to die, doesn't he?" I asked.

"You don't understand," they said. "If we can get you to

wherever he is supposed to be, and if he's not there, keep on until we get you to his side, we can work it out."

Then the head man said, "Mr. Roberts, He hasn't made up his mind if God heals or not, and we've got to slip up on him gradually."

I said, "You know, you men are talking to me as if I were the healer. God is the Source of healing. I'll tell you what God is saying to me while you are talking. He's saying that if this man will stop long enough to hear His Word, meditate upon God and His ways, and start putting God FIRST, there's a good possibility he can be helped both medically and by the prayer of faith. I'm willing to do anything I can, but I am only an instrument of God's healing power, just as a physician is. God is the Source of all healing. It's His conditions we have to meet."

At that point the men got up and left. In my heart I pray for them and for their friend, but as they left that day I could not help but think of Malachi pleading with God's Chosen People to meet His conditions, then He would bless them.

I do not say this in anger. I feel a hurt inside because I know God is saying, "Return unto me and I will return unto you." I know God is the Source and unless you start considering Him as your Source, you are not going to make it.

You are hearing many voices today on television, on radio, in the newspapers and magazines, in public and private, but are you hearing God's voice? Are you developing a *listening* heart?

Listen! Listen! God is saying to you: "Return unto me, and I will return unto you." All of God's promises of blessing are on the condition — "If you will . . . I will."

"CAN YOU READ ME?"

In the days when the telegraph system was new, a call went out for telegraphers. A young man who had learned the dots and dashes of this new communication system applied for the job.

When he arrived for the interview the outer office was filled with other applicants ahead of him. His heart sank. As he stood there, he raised his head and listened, then disappeared behind the door of one of the offices. Soon he came back out. "You can all go home now," he said. "I got the job."

"What do you mean, you got the job? We've been here all morning," the others said.

He replied, "When I came in a few minutes ago I heard a sound. It was dots and dashes being typed out, saying, 'Can you read me? If so, come on in; you have the job!' Well, I can read the dots and dashes of the telegraph system. So I rushed in and they hired me."

My friend, God is communicating with you right now. Are you in need of a miracle? Do you want God to open the windows of heaven? Are you ready to know WHO YOU ARE in God's eyes, so you can start moving toward the FLOOD STAGE of His blessing supply? Then open your heart to His words, "Return unto me, and I will return unto You." Or if you are having a so-so walk with Him, let your faith go to Him for a closer relationship. Get in the stream of God's best for you spiritually, physically, financially.

Now for God's challenge . . .

SUMMED UP

1. How can I count the ways God has loved me?
2. I must see God as my Source so I will be blessed.
3. I can get the curse off my seed if I choose to.
4. Have I left God and don't even know it?
5. I ask myself, "Will I rob God? Will I steal from Him?"
6. Am I cultivating a listening heart so I can "hear" what God is saying to me?
7. Am I ready for God's challenge to me?

Write down what this chapter said to you — right now.

_____

_____

_____

_____

_____

_____

_____

_____

_____

_____

_____

_____

_____

_____

_____

_____

CHAPTER TWELVE

GOD'S CHALLENGE TO YOU: "PROVE ME!"

Bring ye all the tithes and offerings into the store-house, that there may be meat in mine house, and prove me now herewith, saith the Lord of hosts, if I will not open you the windows of heaven, and pour you out a blessing that there shall not be room enough to receive it. — Malachi 3:10

PUTTING GOD'S PROMISES TO the test is a basic biblical theme. Over and over God says, "Come," "taste," "ask," but this is the only place in the Bible where God comes right out and specifically says, "PROVE ME." This is your opportunity to do it.

He says, "Prove me now herewith . . ." You do not have to wait or put it off another minute. You can prove Him "now herewith," starting right where you are.

He says, "Put Me to the test." One man told me that he was afraid to put God to the test. I asked him why. He answered, "What if He doesn't come through? Then I won't have any faith in Him."

I felt like saying, "Brother, you don't have any faith in Him now!"

As far as I am concerned, when you are not sure in your own heart WHO GOD REALLY IS, it causes you to be afraid to prove Him. Without proving God to yourself, you can never know WHO YOU REALLY ARE. The reason so many of us are poor spiritually and financially . . . and are not happy Christians and good witnesses of our Lord, is because we have not proven God like He said for us to do. In fact this may be the first time you actually knew you were supposed to *prove* him.

CHRISTIAN "NO MAN'S LAND"

This "No Man's Land," where Christians are afraid to prove God, is also where all too many live with their fears and frustrations and lack of successful Christian living. Just the idea of trying to prove God turns them off or gives them the jitters. Too many have gotten into a sort of comfortableness of church-going, or occasional church-going, and doing it only because they feel "it's the thing to do." Is this you?

The fact is, God is not really alive to them in a personal, vibrant way. To them, the Bible is hard to understand and whatever happened back there in Bible times has little or no meaning for them in the NOW of their existence. They give the preacher a "good listening," then get up and go home without thinking much about it, or searching the Scriptures for themselves. Does this describe you?

In a way, the church to them is the building, their friends being there, the order of the church service, a place to get married or for their funeral to be preached. When they give, it is without that joyous, decisive, overflowing sense of getting into FLOOD STAGE with God. They don't give "tithes of all" as their own personal Seed-Faith to God, feeling that someone else more able will do it. So they are on a slow merry-go-round, going nowhere and without the most powerful force in the world: the miracle of Seed-Faith at work in their own lives. It's like a cancer eating at them invisibly until it's too late. Clearly something must be done to change this. Here is the answer:

DARE TO PROVE GOD

God said, "Prove me now herewith." Why would God say

that and with such urgency — to PROVE Him and to DO IT NOW?

The answer is that giving our tithes and offerings comes out of the Foundation Faith Abraham had in God — faith based on PROOF. The proof of Abraham's faith came out of WHO GOD WAS to him. Having that proof — or that evidence — led Abraham to know WHO HE WAS and out of that sure knowledge, he "gave tithes of all" and God blessed him in "everything."

You say, "But can I have the same kind of proof or evidence for my faith as Abraham did? Can I dare to prove God as He has told me to?"

Yes, you can have the evidence of WHO GOD IS, and yes, you can dare to prove God to yourself. If this were not so, God would not have told you to prove Him. God is a God of His Word.

In every court of law in the land the judge demands *evidence* on which to render his verdict. Not hearsay, but proven *evidence*.

YOU LIKE A GUARANTEE

When you buy something, you want evidence that it is what it is supposed to be. You like a written guarantee from a reputable company or individual.

If you were asked to take a seat, you would have in your mind evidence that it would support your weight. No matter what would be said about the seat, you would sit on it only if you consciously or unconsciously knew that it would not collapse and cause injury to your body.

Do you think for one second that the Most High God would ask you to prove Him if He didn't have the evidence for your faith to act upon? Listen, God isn't playing with your life. He made you. His Son died for you. He sent His Holy Spirit to live IN you forever. You are the "apple of His eye." He cares for you. And the faith He has given you — a full measure of it (Romans 12:3) — is based on the best evidence ever known.

God says, "Now faith is the evidence" (Hebrews 11:1). Evidence of what? ". . . the evidence of things not seen."

How can you have evidence of things you cannot see? This is where you can bring your faith in God into action. You can release your faith, telling it to come up out of your heart and go to God and find the evidence for what you cannot see.

You cannot see the air, but you have evidence of it because you breathe it into your lungs.

What about gravity? You cannot see it or feel it but you know it is there. Your ability to walk on this earth is to you the evidence of gravity.

THE BANKER

I'm reminded of the man who went to the president of a bank and said, "I have come to get my hundred dollars."

The banker said, "What hundred dollars?"

The man said, "Several months ago you said that if I ever got in need, you would let me have a hundred dollars."

"I don't remember promising you any hundred dollars," replied the banker.

Then the man pulled a piece of paper out of his pocket and said, "Read this."

The banker read, "I promise this man up to one hundred dollars if he ever needs it," and the banker saw that he had signed his name to the paper.

Without hesitation the banker called to the cashier and said, "Let this man have a hundred dollars."

The banker let him have a hundred dollars, not because he simply asked for it, but *because the man had evidence that the banker had promised him the money if he ever needed it.*

You and I have evidence through our faith in God's Word when He says, "Prove me!"

OPENING THE WINDOWS OF HEAVEN

God said, "Prove me now herewith, saith the Lord of hosts, if I will not open you the windows of heaven, and pour you out a blessing [continuously], that there shall not be room enough to contain it."

I want you to feel in your spirit that God is saying this to you personally. Remember in chapter one of this book I opened by asking, "What if you and the Lord were talking together?" Well, God is talking to you now:

> "Bring all your tithes and offerings so there will be resources in My house, and prove Me. I will pour out a blessing upon you (not a curse, but a blessing) — such a blessing that it will be bigger than anything you have to hold it."

I want to remind you that you have been battered, bruised, denied, stolen from, mistreated, fooled, disappointed, disillusioned, let down; and suffered so many defeats that it is hard, very hard, for you to accept God's personal offer, isn't it? I know, for I have felt this way many times too.

How would you like to know you can prove God exactly like He asks you here, then start being blessed so much that you can't carry it all, store it up, or contain it — THAT IT OVERFLOWS YOUR LIFE?

How would you like to plant your tithing seed as God asks you, then have the proof of God multiplying that seed until the end result is so blessed that all the past disappointments and lacks are REPLACED COMPLETELY? That God will give you back all the devil has ever stolen from you?

WHEN GOD SENDS A FLOOD

Notice, God said He himself would pour you out a blessing. Think of a rain — a heavy rain, a downpour.

God said, "I will open the windows of heaven, and I will pour you out a blessing."

Have you ever thought how it would be for the Most High God, Possessor of heaven and earth, and Deliverer from all your enemies, to pour something out?

Picture in your mind God pouring. IT WOULD BE A FLOOD! Otherwise you could contain it, right? Remember, God said there would not be room enough to contain it. SO IT WOULD HAVE TO BE A FLOOD.

Now these words, "I will open the windows of heaven," go back to Genesis 7:10,11. What happened back there?

A FLOOD CAME!

The windows of heaven were opened! It rained forty days and nights, so much that the earth could not contain it. The waters completely filled and overflowed the earth.

God opened the windows of heaven and the rain poured down. It filled the valleys, covered the mountains, and the earth could not contain it.

The Hebrew rabbis tell us that the Hebrew word for "opening the windows of heaven" in Malachi 3:10 is also used in Genesis 7:10,11 when God sent the Flood. They mean the same thing, except in Genesis 7:10,11 God pours out *rain,* and in Malachi 3:10 He pours out *blessing.* Both were poured out in FLOOD STAGE!

This is the kind of blessing God says He will give His people — give you . . . give me.

> He said He himself would do the opening of heaven's windows . . . windows you have shut up against yourself.
>
> He said He himself would do the pouring of the uncontainable blessing . . .
>
> He himself would rebuke the devourer (the devil's power) from destroying you.

Picture in your mind how great a blessing that really is. I have done this many times and I want you to do it. Think of a flood of blessing pouring forth from heaven. You will see it is more than you can contain by any capacities you have.

God is talking to you about a *Flood of Blessing.* He is talking to you about His nature, which when Abraham saw, he declared God is above all and everything. The nature of God is *abundance.*

Remember, one of the reasons Jesus came to the earth as a man was to show us what God is like. Jesus said, "He that hath seen me hath seen the Father" (John 14:9). Paul said, "For in him dwelleth all the fullness of the Godhead bodily" (Colossians 2:9). Jesus also said, "I am come that you might have life, and have it more abundantly" (John 10:10).

Abundance in Abraham's time, *abundance* in Jesus' ministry on earth, *abundance* in God blessing us "now herewith!"

When God blesses you, you are blessed as no one, or nothing else, can bless you.

NOT A TRICKLE, NOT A STREAM, NOT A RIVER, BUT A FLOOD

God didn't say, "I'll open the windows of heaven and pour you out a *trickle!*"

He didn't say, "I'll open the windows of heaven and pour you out a *stream!*"

He didn't say, "I'll open the windows of heaven and pour you out a *river!*"

God said, "I'll open the windows of heaven and pour you out a FLOOD!"

Some people are in the desert stage of life. Some are in the *trickle* stage of God's blessings. Some are in the *stream* stage of His blessings. Others are trying to get into the *river* stage of His blessings. But how many are in the FLOOD STAGE?

In a recent seminar I conducted at Oral Roberts University, with about 2,200 people present, I asked how many were in that FLOOD STAGE of God's blessings and were unable to contain the blessings that God had poured out upon them. Eight people stood up. Out of 2,200 Christians, only eight were in the FLOOD STAGE!

I asked how many were in the *river* stage. About 50 stood up.

When I asked how many were in the *stream* stage, about 150 stood up.

But when I asked how many were in the *trickle* stage, the remaining 2,000 people stood up.

No wonder they were in the trickle stage. They did not yet understand WHO GOD IS. They were not giving tithes of all as their Seed-Faith to God, like Abraham did, and therefore were not in the position, as Abraham was, to expect God to "multiply their seed exceedingly."

In that seminar we began to learn WHO GOD IS — that He is the Most High God, Possessor of heaven and earth, Deliverer from all our enemies, the One we worship with our tithes and offerings as Seed-Faith. When the people realized this, they saw the three Keys of the Miracle of Seed-Faith.

> **First,** God is my Source. **Second,** I will plant my seed out of my need, giving my best and giving it first. **Third,** I will expect God to multiply my seed sown that I may reap my harvests, both naturally and supernaturally.

They began to grasp these three Keys of the Miracle of Seed-Faith because they wanted in on the FLOOD STAGE of God's blessings! No wonder so many keep coming to these seminars year after year. As they absorb God's Holy Word on living in the rhythm of the Seed-Faith life, and continue releasing their faith for their miracle harvests God grows for them, they begin to enter FLOOD STAGE. These dear Seed-Faith partners are the happiest people I know. It's a joy to be around them because they are being BLESSED and MADE A BLESSING.

Seed-Faith is so old it sounds new. It began in Genesis 3:15. It was . . .

- restored after the Flood (Genesis 8:22),
- proven by Abraham (Genesis 14:18-20; 24:1),
- set in motion as God's multiplication system for our lives "as long as earth remains,"
- continued by Jesus (Matthew 17:20; Luke 6:38), and
- explained by St. Paul (II Corinthians 9:10; Galatians 6:7-9; Philippians 4:15-19).

Speaking from proven personal experience, the greatest miracle after the saving of our souls is the MIRACLE OF SEED-FAITH. I would not attempt to live without it. It has opened me up to believe for God's FLOOD STAGE of blessings for me and thousands of my friends and partners.

SUMMED UP

1. I thank God that He is so real He invites me to "prove Him," getting evidence for my faith to act upon things not seen.
2. My giving tithes and offerings as a seed for God to multiply takes me back to Foundation Faith.
3. God is speaking to me personally that He wants to open the windows of heaven to me.
4. The nature of God is abundance . . . Jesus said He came to give life to me more abundantly.
5. I want not a trickle, not a stream, not a river, but a FLOOD of God's blessings.
6. I thank God I can use the three Miracle Keys of Seed-Faith.
7. I rejoice that at last I have discovered the Seed-Faith principle which runs all through the Word of God.

What does this chapter say to you? Write it down.

_____

_____

_____

_____

_____

_____

_____

_____

_____

_____

_____

_____

_____

_____

_____

CHAPTER THIRTEEN

HOW THE SUCCESS OF YOUR LIFE IS IN GIVING/LIVING

I can do all things through Christ which strengtheneth me . . . My God shall supply all your need according to his riches in glory by Christ Jesus. — Philippians 4:13, 19

WELL, AT LAST! We have reached the New Testament. Doubtless you thought we never would. But at least by now you know that our New Testament faith goes back to Abraham's faith — not just to Abraham, but to his faith, which is our Foundation Faith and from which our Source, Jesus Christ, came. It is also the faith in which is the success of our GIVING/LIVING.

For example, in New Testament days, when Paul came to the city of Philippi to lead people to Christ and teach them how to live by faith, the thrust of his teaching was in "giving and receiving" — or GIVING/LIVING — which will bring you into FLOOD STAGE blessings.

The people of the Philippian Church were very poor. They were defeated in their own eyes, and Paul gave them the straightforward gospel of abundant and victorious living in Jesus Christ. Their response was electric; whereas, in Galatians and in II Corinthians, Paul had to URGE Christians to SOW and REAP. In writing to the Christians at Philippi, all he

As you study God's Word, as this partner is doing, you can know both WHO GOD IS and then WHO YOU ARE IN HIM. It was a great day in my life in 1947 when I finally had studied the Bible sufficiently to understand that God is totally good and the devil is totally bad.

had to do was simply REMIND them of the power of GIV-ING/LIVING.

The heart of what he said is in the following seven verses, which I have committed to memory. I hope you will read and re-read each part, then study it as a whole so you can refer to it again and again as you reach with your faith toward GIVING/ LIVING.

I can do all things through Christ which strengtheneth me. Nothwithstanding ye have well done, that ye did communicate with my affliction. Now ye Philippians know also, that in the beginning of the gospel, when I departed from

*Macedonia, no church communicated with me as
concerning giving and receiving, but ye only. For
even in Thessalonica ye sent once and again unto
my necessity. Not because I desire a gift: but I
desire fruit that may abound to your account. But
I have all, and abound: I am full, having received
of Epaphroditus the things which were sent from
you, an odour of a sweet smell, a sacrifice
acceptable, well-pleasing to God. But my God
shall supply all your need according to his riches
in glory by Christ Jesus* (Philippians 4:13-19).

St. Paul started everything he did with giving — as plant-ing a seed. And he taught us to do the same. To Paul, the way to "receiving" God's abundance began with "giving," which is the same principle Abraham used in "giving tithes of all" and being "blessed in everything."

Paul knew that what you give to God comes back multiplied according to God's riches, not merely man's. And it comes back through Christ Jesus who, after His death and resurrec-tion, ascended to heaven and reclaimed all the riches He had laid aside to be born as a man: to sit where we sit, to feel what we feel, and to give the benefits of salvation both on EARTH and in HEAVEN (Ephesians 1:20-22).

Nothing could stop Paul. Not persecution, misrepresenta-tion, jail, or whippings, or opposition of any kind, for he said, *"I can do all things through Christ which strengtheneth me."*

Now have you ever opened your mind and your life to what St. Paul taught about how you are to be a CAN-DO person in this world, and one whose needs are supplied — not accord-ing to any human measurement, but by God's own riches? What I am about to share now, spiritually and financially, changed my life. It has given me the ability to go beyond myself and do things for God greater than I had thought possible . . . and to do it by my SEED-FAITHING, which began in Abraham and continued through the children of Israel. It was practiced by Jesus himself and was followed by the Christians of the early churches who were successful in their Christian living on this earth.

One thing for certain is shown by Paul and the Christians at Philippi, they stopped the devil from damming up the flow of God's riches for the meeting of all their NEEDS. We see them in FLOOD STAGE.

LIKE TWO SLICES OF BREAD

Read verse 13: "*I can do all things through Christ which strengtheneth me.*" Then skip through to verse 19: "*My God shall supply all your need according to His riches in glory by Christ Jesus.*"

Most Christians can quote these two scriptures by memory, but they fail to connect verses 13 and 19 together with what is said in between. Verses 13 and 19 are like the two slices of bread for a sandwich, but the other verses are the meat between.

For centuries, it has been like Christians have had two slices of bread spiritually, physically, and financially . . . but almost totally without the SUBSTANCE within to make the whole sandwich, or to make their health and wholeness in spirit, mind, body, and finances really happen.

The *trigger* for your faith is NOT in verses 13 or 19. It is in verses 14 through 19, for it is in those verses that Paul put giving AND receiving together, putting the meat between the two slices of bread.

At every point when Paul taught on giving, he connected it with the principle of the seed — and with SEEDTIME AND HARVEST. You see this in his teaching in Galatians 6:7, "For whatsoever a man soweth, that shall he also reap." He is saying, "You SOW it, God will GROW it, and you will REAP IT."

In Philippians 4:15,16 he said, "When I departed from Macedonia [the region where Philippi was located], no church communicated with me as concerning giving and receiving, but ye only." He added, "For . . . ye sent once and again unto my necessity," meaning again and again.

Many Christians in other places had not yet learned to apply this eternal principle of giving and receiving — seedtime and harvest, sowing and reaping — as those in Philippi did FROM THE VERY BEGINNING OF BECOMING CHRISTIANS under the ministry of St. Paul.

Some people who receive Christ as their personal Savior immediately think, "Now I am a Christian, and when I die I will go to heaven," which is true. Others, upon receiving Christ, go on to learn His eternal principles that cause them to see Him as the One whose name God has exalted above everything that is named in *this* world, as well as the world to come (Ephesians 1:20,21). They learn . . .

- that "the Son of God was manifested, that he might destroy the works of the devil" in our lives (I John 3:8),
- that He multiplies the seed sown exceedingly, giving the blessing of Abraham: "Surely blessing I will bless thee, and multiplying I will multiply thee" (Hebrews 6:14), and
- that it is in our giving that we TRIGGER our receiving, just as in sowing a farmer triggers the harvest that he is to receive.

The Christians in Philippi wanted a RELATIONSHIP with Christ *and* with His servant Paul, who was the messenger of Christ and had brought the gospel to them. In this relationship they started *giving*, believing Paul's teaching of the Word of God that *receiving* would always *follow* their *giving*. Just as Paul had taught that "giving and receiving" belong together, their *giving and receiving* became a rhythm of their faith in operation . . . like the rhythm of *breathing out and breathing in.*

Now I want you to make a little experiment. First, breathe OUT. Second, breathe IN. Next, breathe OUT again and hold it! Hold it!

Are you out of breath? Yes? There's only one thing you can do to keep breathing, and that is AFTER you have breathed all your breath OUT, to breathe it in AGAIN. Right?

You breathe out, you breathe in; you breathe out, you breathe in. You get into a rhythm of breathing out and breathing in — or you will die!

Paul is saying, there is a rhythm in your giving and receiving. He doesn't say, Give only; nor does he say, Receive only. He says "giving AND receiving," doing it in rhythm or you will fail utterly in the eternal principle of the seed: seedtime and harvest, sowing and reaping, giving and receiving, and being loved by God as "a cheerful giver." You can never be a cheerful giver unless you are also a regular reaper/receiver. The rhythm of giving and receiving must be there at all times in your GIVING/LIVING.

THE SOFT DRINK MACHINE

Let me illustrate in another way how RHYTHM is so important to you in your giving and receiving!

One day I stood before a soft drink machine, waiting my turn. I watched others put in their coins, then automatically reach down for the can to come out. Every time they gave their coins to the machine, it gave up the can containing the soft drink. It was a rhythm of giving the coins, then reaching down to receive the can.

Then I realized that they were doing this without a doubt in the world. Consciously or unconsciously they knew a contract existed between themselves, the maker of the machine, and the suppliers of the cans of soft drinks. Therefore, when they put in the coins they reached down to receive — or get — the can. When they gave their coins to the soft drink machine, they automatically expected to receive something back — and they got it.

When the Philippian Christians gave, they expected a miracle — the miracle of receiving back from God. Their giving to God was to the local church, also to Paul and his evangelistic missionary team. But they expected their receiving to come from God, their Source. They did this so regularly that they got into a rhythm of *giving and receiving* because they had a relationship with God and His messenger Paul — a partnership that worked!

Paul shows us that the benefits of our relationship with the Lord are in our "giving and receiving." In other words, as he said in Galatians 6:7 — we SOW it, God GROWS it, and we REAP it, drawing upon both God's natural and supernatural supply.

Make no mistake about it, there is *receiving* in heaven. But there is also *receiving* here on earth. And all the receiving in heaven and in earth is from the same Source our giving goes to — God.

To us who are Christians, learning God's Source System, God's Financial System, and God's Blessing System — and working in rhythm with it day by day — makes the difference in our success as a child of God. It means to us as it did to Abraham that God BLESSES us to MAKE us a BLESSING.

WHY SOW?

An opportunity to give is an opportunity to receive. Paul gave the Philippian Christians the opportunity to give: "Not because I desire a gift, but I desire fruit that may abound to YOUR account" (Philippians 4:17). Notice Paul wanted them to have "fruit."

Fruit comes from seed — seed that has been planted. Unless Paul had instructed that through their seed planting they would have fruit in abundance — or ABOUNDING — they would not have been aware that they could build an account with God through having a relationship with Him as their . . .

SOURCE SYSTEM,
FINANCIAL SYSTEM,
BLESSING SYSTEM.

Unless Paul had taught them "giving and receiving," they would not have EXPECTED TO RECEIVE. He wanted them to know that their giving produced receiving, that they were to be constantly getting miracle harvests from the seeds of faith they planted. In this way they would be building an account with God from which they would be able to continually receive spiritually, physically, financially.

AND WHERE?

Paul said of their giving to him, "Not that I desire a gift."

No man or woman of God can go around expecting personal gifts. But Jesus says, "The laborer is worthy of his hire" (Luke 10:7), and Paul says, "Thou shalt not muzzle the mouth of the ox that treadeth out the corn" (I Corinthians 9:9).

When God's minister gives himself or herself to the gospel, those who benefit through the ministry should give to him in the same way the Philippian Christians gave to Paul who said of their giving, "I have all and abound, having received . . . the things which were sent from you" (Philippians 4:18). Because Paul's finances abounded in him, he could further help them to trust God to supply all their needs.

The inference Paul gives here is, how can a preacher of the gospel whose own financial needs are not met inspire the faith of others to believe for the money they must have? At the same time the preacher must never "desire a gift" as his highest priority, but rather seek the financial blessings of God for His people. The preacher's "giving and receiving" will work for him or her in the same way it does for lay Christians.

Paul put the highest value on preaching the Word of God. He said that as you hear the Word preached your "faith cometh" (Romans 10:17). The more you really "hear" preaching by your spirit and mind (if it is preached under the anointing of the Holy Spirit), the more faith you will have to believe that God is Most High God, Possessor of heaven and earth, Deliverer from all your enemies, Multiplier of the seed sown, and the more you will enter into "giving and receiving," as the Philippian Christians did.

It is thought that Paul was in a Roman jail when he wrote to the Philippians. The brother who brought their gifts to him again and again was not ashamed of Paul's sufferings for the gospel, and did not think that excused him and the other Christians from giving to God's minister. He knew in their giving they would receive. They would build a financial reservoir with God, and fruit would abound to their account.

This is why we give friends and partners of this ministry an opportunity to give. It may be a special project to sponsor by their Seed-Faith gifts. It may be some part of the City of Faith, or helping send an ORU missionary Healing Team, or furnishing a dorm room at ORU, or giving to the television and radio programs, or giving to some other phase of the ministry. We teach them to give out of their need to receive from God, to give their best in order to expect to receive God's best, and to give first, for scriptural giving is always a seed . . . and a seed is always sown first or there will be no harvest to reap.

Some of these friends and partners are church people, some are not. Some have never received Christ. And we always attempt to help them receive Christ as their personal Savior, then urge them to return to church and be an active part of the Body of Christ, planting their seeds of faith regularly and rhythmically in harmony with God's system.

We don't ask them to "seed" only to this ministry but to give to their local church too, especially if that church is preaching, teaching, and healing as Jesus said. Also, to give to other faith ministries as they are led of God. Certainly we are not the only ministry doing God's work.

These dear friends and partners are not our Source, and we are not their Source. God is the Source of each of us. And whenever and wherever each of us plants our seed in God's work, we will do it joyously. We know that Jesus' Name is above every name. He controls both the natural and supernatural sources of supply. He is our Deliverer spiritually, physically, and financially — here and in the life to come. He is all in all to us . . . and He multiplies our seed sown. We SOW it, God GROWS it, we REAP it (Galatians 6:7).

PAUL KNEW GOD'S FINANCIAL SYSTEM

Paul was brilliantly trained in the Old Covenant, knowing the faith of Abraham intimately and clearly. He knew and understood God's Financial System as it operated in Malachi 3:10,11, where God commanded that the tithes and offerings be brought into the storehouse so He could pour out a blessing on the people.

As Paul interpreted Abraham's giving "tithes of all" in Genesis 14:20, and Malachi 3:10,11 AFTER Jesus fulfilled the Old Covenant, he saw that the giving of Christians would cause God to show forth the same goodness He gave to Abraham in *blessing* and *making* him a *blessing*. God would become personally involved with them in their needs by opening the windows of heaven, which their nongiving had shut up against them, and POUR them out FLOOD STAGE blessings

— uncontainable blessings which would flood their lives, giving them God's abundance.

In the New Testament, under the risen living Christ, who dwelt in him by His Spirit, Paul put the FLOOD STAGE of Malachi 3:10,11 in three words: GIVING AND RECEIVING. The tithes and offerings, given under the Old Covenant as seed to be multiplied, were emphasized even more as seed under the New Covenant. To us Christians, our giving is truly Seed-Faith.

Our giving is the *trigger* for us to receive back in a measure ACCORDING TO GOD'S RICHES BY CHRIST JESUS IN HEAVEN. The opening of the windows of heaven of Malachi 3:10 becomes the *inexhaustible* in Philippians 4:19! "My God shall supply all your need" — the supply shall never be exhausted because it comes from the riches of God himself.

In the Old Testament, giving all of the tithes and offerings caused God to open the windows of heaven and pour out UNCONTAINABLE blessings; and in the New Testament, our giving puts us in the FLOOD STAGE of the INEXHAUSTIBLE!

Establishing your rhythm of *giving and receiving,* of *sowing and reaping,* enables you to truly know WHO JESUS IS and WHO YOU ARE in Jesus: one whose need is supplied "according to God's riches in glory by Christ Jesus." Jesus, according to Paul, is intimately involved with you and your need being met by His inexhaustible riches. FLOOD STAGE RICHES!

God possesses the heaven and the earth — the natural and the supernatural — and He doesn't make a difference in one or the other. Neither should you nor I. Whether He supplies our needs naturally or supernaturally, or by both, it makes no difference: both belong to God and to us!

GIVING/LIVING is what your relationship with Christ is

all about. Paul in Philippians 4:18 says our giving and receiving is . . .

> "an odour of a sweet smell,
>   a sacrifice acceptable,
>   well-pleasing to God."

When Paul says it is "well-pleasing to God," he is speaking of our giving and receiving — by faith. Hebrews 11:6 says, "Without faith it is impossible to please [God]." When we have faith in God, we are to use it to "give and receive," so that our Seed-Faith pleases God, making it "well-pleasing to Him."

You can no more serve God without faith than you can breathe without breath; you can no more receive without giving than you can breathe in, without breathing out.

Paul said in Philippians 4:13, "I can do all things . . ." It sounds like he is bragging, doesn't it? This is the same Paul who when he first met Christ was so confused and lost that he couldn't do anything right. Now he says in all truth that he could "do ALL THINGS through Christ which strengtheneth me," or "through Christ who is my Source."

He follows that by showing that "giving and receiving" is the trigger to being a CAN-DO person. In verse 19, he says we can have a DESIRED RESULT through our "giving and receiving."

But my God . . . Here Paul personalizes God: MY God. Not God just to someone else, but GOD TO ME. *Shall supply all [my] need* . . . MY need. Again he personalizes. This time it's his — our — personal need being supplied.

Friend, put your faith on these truths of God. Know your Seed-Faith rights and stand on them.

There are only two more chapters . . . they may be the most important of all to you IF you have prepared yourself by reading straight through from chapter one, getting back to your Source, getting into the sweep of God's moving in men, understanding the establishment of God as your Source and the system by which He works in you, and getting into the flow of FLOOD STAGE.

I am eagerly awaiting the blessing you will receive from the final two chapters . . .

SUMMED UP

1. Paul sharply brings to my attention that my success is in GIVING/LIVING.

2. As Paul started everything he did by giving (sowing a seed), so I will follow God's eternal principle of the seed.

3. I can be a CAN-DO Christian through my "giving and receiving," just as I have physical life through my breathing out, then breathing in.

4. I remind myself that Philippians 4:13 and 4:19 belong together . . . and that all between is the "meat" between the two slices of bread.

5. I will not forget the experience of the soft drink machine.

6. I am to give, then expect to receive, in this life and the life to come. My opportunity to give is my opportunity to receive according to God's riches for "all" my need.

7. My FLOOD STAGE of Malachi 3:10,11 is my inexhaustible in Philippians 4:19.

8. I will be a CAN-DO Christian, trusting God for FLOOD STAGE blessings.

Write down what this chapter said to you — right now.

_____

_____

_____

_____

_____

_____

_____

_____

_____

_____

_____

_____

_____

_____

_____

_____

_____

_____

CHAPTER FOURTEEN

HOW TO STOP THE DEVIL FROM STEALING YOUR MONEY

The thief cometh not, but for to steal, and to kill,
and to destroy: I am come that they might have
life, and that they might have it more abundantly.
— John 10:10

THE ARCHANGEL LUCIFER BECAME the devil because he stole from God and tried to take over God's throne. God stopped him by throwing him out of heaven. When the devil, being cast to earth, saw that he could no longer rob God directly, he began to rob God's creatures, especially man.

Satan knew that God in creating man had made him in His own image and likeness, making him a spiritual being to live in a human body on the earth, with the power to subdue and replenish it (Genesis 1:28). He also knew that man, as God's masterpiece, had the widest powers of expression and worship. By setting about to rob man of his worship of God and the things over which God made him ruler, the devil felt he could strike a blow at God again. Actually, the battle over man is not man against man; it is a battle of the devil against God to see which one of them man will worship and serve.

What does this titanic battle between God and the devil have to do with your money? You will soon see.

THE BATTLE BETWEEN GOD AND THE DEVIL

God stopped the devil from robbing Him directly. But He

can only stop the devil from robbing you when you inform yourself from God's Word that the devil's very purpose in coming to you is only "to steal, and to kill, and to destroy" your life and all that is precious to you (John 10:10).

St. Paul, who fought against the devil, refusing to be robbed by him, said, "We are not ignorant of [the devil's] devices" (II Corinthians 2:11). You, too, must see to it that you are keenly aware of the devil's ways.

Since the battle over your life is between God and the devil, you must continue to study God's Word so you will know both WHO GOD IS and who the devil is, and what the purpose of both is toward you.

It was a great day in my life in 1947 when I finally had studied the Bible sufficiently to understand that God is totally good and the devil is totally bad. John 10:10 became the focal point from which I was able to see the devil as a thief, robber, and destroyer — and to see Jesus as coming to give to me — us — life and to give it *more abundantly.*

I saw that God and the devil are total opposites and that the devil is no match for God anytime, anywhere, or in any way. "Greater is he [God] that is in you, than he [the devil] that is in the world" (I John 4:4). That scripture rang in my ears. Every time we say it or sing it on our television program, a thrill of victory over the devil surges through me. Our God is greater than the devil! God knows He is greater, you and I must know it too. We can strengthen our faith enormously by knowing we can win over the devil and take back what he has stolen from us.

You must ask yourself three questions: (1) *How is the devil stealing from me?* (2) *How can I stop him from stealing what I have?* (3) *How can I get back what he has stolen from me?* Let me share with you what I believe the Bible teaches and what I have personally experienced in answering these three most important questions.

HOW THE DEVIL STEALS FROM YOU

Understand that the devil is seeking to rob you of giving tithes and offerings for God to open the windows of heaven so He can prosper you in FLOOD STAGE and rebuke the devil's destroying power over you (Malachi 3:10,11).

When Abraham gave "tithes of all," one of the first things he experienced was the power of the supernatural to come down from heaven and multiply his seed exceedingly. The barrenness of his wife, Sarah, was healed by the supernatural power of God coming upon both of them in their natural old age and renewing their power to conceive and bring forth a son, Isaac (Genesis 21:1,2).

So the first thing the devil seeks to steal from you is the RELATIONSHIP of your tithes and offerings as DIVINE SEED for the almighty God to multiply exceedingly *in every part of your life,* including the money that RIGHTFULLY belongs to you.

The devil wants you to believe the giving of tithes and offerings is not seed for God to multiply, neither does he want it to be an act of your recognizing WHO GOD IS and WHO YOU ARE. Nor does he want you to believe it is a supreme act of your worship of God. Instead, the devil wants you to believe that when you give you are giving something away, and that you are a fool for giving, since it only diminishes what you have.

Therefore, the devil tries to steal your *desire* to give to God, making you think you will be worse off instead of having the knowing of your faith that God will BLESS you and MAKE you a BLESSING.

THE LOVE OF MONEY IS THE ROOT OF ALL EVIL

St. Paul says, "The love of money is the root of all evil" (I Timothy 6:10). Not money itself, but the LOVE of it — the lust for it.

Satan, according to Ezekiel 28:13,14, was once in the Garden of Eden where he possessed every precious stone as well as all the gold. One of his supreme delights was to walk "up and down in the midst of the stones of fire" — meaning the diamonds, sapphires, emeralds, onyx, and jasper, etc. This represented financial and social power to him and he transformed this false representation to the fallen Adam, and through Adam to his organic descendants to this day. He either tries to make Christians believe money is their source, rather than God who owns all the money and precious gems, or he seeks to make us believe we are not supposed to have God's wealth.

Moses said, "It is [God] who giveth thee power to get wealth" (Deuteronomy 8:18). He had given that power first to the archangel Lucifer, who had greedily taken this power to attempt to rob God of His very throne. By allowing *the love of money* to possess him, that "money love" became the root of all the evil he has ever done. The love of money became the root or seed for all his desire to destroy God and His creation.

On the other hand, you must clearly understand from the Bible that the power to get money is God-given and is therefore a *holy thing*. But the *love*, or *lusting*, for it originated in the devil, and contaminates every person who allows it to take hold of him. It is an evil seed. The devil's purpose is to confuse the power to get money with the *love* of it, so that it will ultimately destroy you.

Make no mistake about it, all evil you have ever done originated from lusting after money, rather than longing to know God. Yet God tells you plainly . . .

- *that "the earth is the Lord's, and the fulness thereof"* (Psalm 24:1);
- *that all "the silver and gold" are His* (Haggai 2:8);
- *that He wishes ABOVE ALL THINGS that*

you "prosper . . . even as your soul pros-
pers" (III John 2);

- that if you seek God and His kingdom first,
"all these THINGS shall be ADDED unto
you" (Luke 12:31); and
- that as you get into His system of "giving
and receiving," He will "supply all your
needs according to his riches" (Philippians
4:19).

Please read and re-read this paragraph until it becomes part of
your believing and thinking.

Money is NOT evil, or God wouldn't be rich with it. Having
wealth is not evil, or God would not give "power to get
wealth." Money is evil only if you are evil; wealth is bad only if
you lust for it and use it in a way that does not glorify God.

God knows that money represents power in the earth; that
is one of the reasons He put it here. Therefore, He wishes
above all things that our MONEY PROSPERITY equal our
SPIRITUAL PROSPERITY (III John 2). This equality is part
of our wholeness as sons and daughters of Abraham . . . and as
Christian believers. God knows IF and WHEN we accept
that dual prosperity as being BLESSED of Him, we then can
submit ourselves to BE MADE A BLESSING, the same as
Abraham was BLESSED and submitted himself to be MADE
A BLESSING.

THE WORLD SYSTEM PERVERTS GOD'S MONEY SYSTEM

Abraham knew God was the Most High God, Possessor of
heaven and earth, Deliverer from all his enemies; and he gave
tithes of all and, through this, he loved God above and beyond
money and all the power it represented.

Money to Abraham originated in God. God was the Source
of all money; therefore, he associated money with God and
not with the devil. His love for God caused him to look upon
money as coming directly from God, his Source, and not man

except as an instrument. He refused to let the king of Sodom make him rich lest the glory be taken from the Most High God, or that he himself would separate the getting of money from God as his *Source*.

Abraham, by his faith, which is the Foundation Faith for our Christian faith through Jesus Christ our Savior, communicated God's ownership of money to his seed (descendants). And we, who are his spiritual sons and daughters today, freely accept God's ownership of all things. This includes money which the world has made as its power base. But as Christians with a right relationship with God and money, we see this world system as perverting — or misusing — God's money system. The devil through this world system robs God, misuses His money and gives the credit to himself for his ability to get money and manipulate people with it, even causing people to kill for it.

All too often, we have allowed the devil to get away with tempting us to believe wrongly about money. We look at the people of this world system, controlling at least 95 percent of the money, and inwardly feel, "Well, there's nothing I can do about this. I guess if God wanted me to have money He would give it to me." My friend, that is totally unscriptural . . . and stupid.

Instead of using our faith to know WHO GOD IS, then know WHO WE ARE because we are in Christ, and planting our seeds of faith with God as our Source System, our Financial System, and our Blessing System, we often say when we are out of money, "Why me, Lord?" We have a tendency to blame God for the little we have in comparison to what this world has, when it all belongs to God, our Heavenly Father; and through our "giving and receiving," He will supply all our needs according to His RICHES.

When we get into Seed-Faith and begin to prosper, people of the world system burn with jealousy, while at the same time they knock their brains out to live in fine homes, drive the most expensive cars, control the largest businesses, and manipulate the money supply. They act like they think they are God. It's high time we did something positive about our covenant rights regarding our money.

It thrills me when I see a person using his faith in God to prosper, for I know he is walking in the steps of Abraham's faith (Romans 4:12). It thrills me when I see a church packed with people, sinners getting saved, the Holy Spirit being poured out, and money coming in — for I know that kind of church is like the churches of the New Testament that trusted God to bless them spiritually, physically, and financially. As a church man, an ordained elder, I am giving my best to the church, the Body of Christ, to help it come into its full inheritance in every way, including the money it must have!

RECOVERING WHAT THE DEVIL STOLE FROM YOU

There is an extra miracle in your seed planting and that is the *seed of an equal benefit.*

The devil steals and at times he is going to steal from you, especially when you are not wise to his ways.

Every time the devil steals from me (and who doesn't he steal from?), I try to get my faith in action as soon as I discover my loss. No matter how little or how much I have left, I immediately take the best of it and give it as Seed-Faith for God to grow into a harvest that will not only cover my loss, but will give me an even larger benefit.

Remember when the devil stole from the man Job (*Jobe*), he believed God and God "gave him twice as much as he had before" (Job 42:10).

You say, "Oral Roberts, why do you let Satan steal from you?" Well, the devil through Judas stole money from Jesus, as well as betrayed Him (John 12:6). In this life things like this are going to happen but God provides us with the seed of an equal benefit — or even double — if we will only plant it . . . and do it in faith, expecting a miracle return.

One of the worst losses I have suffered came within an inch of wiping out this ministry. It wasn't something I had done bad, either. It came because I was obeying God by launching out in faith, and the devil feared the results.

To cover the loss we had to sell something we owned. At the last hour the Lord impressed me again as He had been doing for days to "give it as a seed I sow to Him." It wasn't easy to sow this seed because the devil was tempting me to believe if I did we would lose everything. But you know what? I sowed this seed as my topmost best seed. Six months passed before God's "due season" came (Galatians 6:9), and almost overnight the entire loss was recovered and we were off and running with a greater anointing and ministry!

Before you go to the final and climactic chapter, I want to urge you to fall in love with God so much that you start getting madder and madder at the devil.

I urge you to accept God's ownership of everything you need and to deny the devil and any rights he claims.

I urge you to use your faith to command the devil to release the money — and other things — he has stolen from you.

I urge you to ask God to send His angels, who are ministering spirits FOR you (Hebrews 1:14), to take from the devil what is yours and give it back to you.

Remember you are a son, or a daughter, of Abraham — and an heir of Abraham and his Foundation Faith. Then remember you are "in Christ," whose Name God has exalted above everything that is named in this world and the world to come — and has put the devil and all things under His feet (Ephesians 1:21,22).

You are on your way to being a winner through Jesus Christ!

As you turn to chapter fifteen, the final one, I ask you to

open yourself up completely so you can really begin working with God's system 100 percent to live and flow in FLOOD STAGE.

SUMMED UP

1. I understand the battle over my life is not between me and a person or a thing. It is a battle between God and the devil — and I can choose which one will win!

2. I see that the devil's only purpose is to steal . . . kill . . . and destroy — including me. God's purpose is to give me more abundant life. Therefore, God and the devil are total opposites.

3. The devil seeks to rob me by tempting me not to give my tithes and offerings so God can open the windows of heaven to me. I give because I want to be like God, and not the devil; and for God to bless me and make me a blessing.

4. I will plant a seed of equal benefit for God to restore what the devil has been stealing from me. I trust God to send His angels to minister for me.

5. I want my full share of God's money, but I will not love it or lust for it. I will trust God who gives me power to fill my financial need.

6. I am God's child and His property, an heir of God; therefore, I take my authority over the devil to stop stealing from me.

7. I am determined to use my faith to work with God's system.

What does this chapter say to you? Write it down.

_____

_____

_____

_____

_____

_____

_____

_____

_____

_____

_____

_____

_____

_____

_____

_____

_____

_____

CHAPTER FIFTEEN

HOW TO WORK WITH GOD'S SYSTEM SO IT WILL WORK WITH YOU SPIRITUALLY PHYSICALLY FINANCIALLY

ONE OF THE BEST WAYS I know to work with God's system so it will work with you is to believe these nine words by memorizing and saying them to yourself until they are part of you:

WITHOUT GOD, I CANNOT.
WITHOUT ME, HE WILL NOT.

Here is the way I say them concerning myself:

WITHOUT GOD, ORAL CANNOT.
WITHOUT ORAL, GOD WILL NOT.

As I come to the end of this book, I have been saying them like this:

GOD AND YOU.
GOD AND ORAL.
GOD AND US.
WORKING TOGETHER,
WE WILL DO IT!

Another way to work with God's system is to do exactly what God said to do to PROVE Him by giving Him all our tithes and offerings, giving them as good seeds. Then He will:

1. Take the curse off our blessings (make things work for us).
2. Purify the seed we SOW for Him to GROW and for us to REAP (putting us in a state of expectancy).
3. Open the windows of heaven to us (windows that are now closed).
4. Pour us out a blessing where there is not room enough to contain it — a Flood! (the very blessing we need).
5. Rebuke the devourer for our sakes (stop the devil from stealing from us).
6. Make us a delightsome person . . . and people (make us an inspiration to other people.)
7. *Bless* us and *make* us a *blessing* (give meaning to our lives).

God very clearly said we are to do the PROVING of Him, and He is to do the OPENING of our closed windows and the POURING out of our blessings in FLOOD STAGE.

You have to make a quality decision today to prove God to yourself. No matter how others have proved God to themselves, God told you to PROVE Him to yourself. I assure you that God is very practically provable and that He will bless and take you

from the Trickle,
from the Stream,
from the River,
to FLOOD STAGE!

This is how others will see God through you and become concerned for themselves to know that God is a good God, and is *always* a good God. Unless we prove God to ourselves, we are unable to demonstrate His goodness to others.

This is so important that I challenge you, just as I do myself, to make this quality decision by an act of your faith that you will take God at His word to test His Source System, His Financial System, and His Blessing System. God established himself — and nothing we can do can cause Him to cease to be. God established the system by which He blesses you and me and all people — and nothing we can do will change that system.

We — you and I — can choose to work with God's system or choose to work against it. We can ignore God's system but it will not go away. This world system of man will change and keep on changing because it is unreliable. Although we have to deal with man's system, we can choose NOT to make it our Source. God and His system is our Source and we can be absolutely sure God and His system will never change . . . and will never fail us. Remember, God will not change His system to fit us, we must change to fit it.

HOW TO WORK WITH GOD'S SYSTEM

First, work spiritually with God's system.

You do this by accepting that God created you in His own image and likeness and made you a living spirit. You are a spirit; therefore, you are first and last a spiritual being.

You are the person inside your body, not the other way around. You have a body but you are not physical. You have a mind but you are not mental. You are spiritual. Therefore everything that touches you touches you first in your spirit. You respond as the spiritual being you are.

God, your Creator, sent Jesus Christ to be your personal Savior and Lord that you may be a reborn child of God. Repent — change your mind about God and yourself by knowing WHO GOD IS, then through knowing Him, know WHO YOU ARE — and as an act of supreme worship of God "give tithes of all," and give as a seed you plant.

This is the way you spiritually enter into Abraham's Foundation Faith and walk in the steps of his faith right into the steps of Jesus who takes you into the New Covenant, a better covenant based upon better promises (Hebrews 8:6).

Second, work physically with God's system.

Whatever affects you physically affects you spiritually, touching your inner man which is your real self.

Therefore, learn about your physical body and how to treat it. Remember, Jesus lived on earth 33 years in a physical body. If your physical body were not important, Jesus would not have lived in a body that was physical, just as yours and mine are.

St. Paul wrote under the inspiration of God: "Your body is the temple of the Holy Spirit which is in you, which ye have of God, and ye are not your own. For ye are bought with a price [Christ's shed blood at Calvary]: therefore glorify God in your body, and in your spirit, which are God's" (I Corinthians 6:19,20).

Hear it inside you: your physical body is the dwelling place — the temple — of God the Holy Spirit. That makes you and your body not your own, but God's property. Both your body and spirit belong to God.

Whatever affects you physically affects you spiritually and mentally, and it also affects God the Holy Spirit, who lives in you as His temple.

Think of God living in your body and making your body a holy instrument in which to live and do His work and in which you live and do your work.

Remember how intertwined your spirit and body are. Many of our best physicians believe some 85 percent of all physical ailments come through the stress or disharmony of your spiritual self. But based on my 34 years of a healing ministry in praying for hundreds of thousands of sick people, I call to your attention that it works the other way around, also.

Your spiritual being is affected dramatically by *the stress and illness of your body.*

Yes, your body can transmit to your spirit — and mind — the pain and damage that is going on in it, which means you must seek healing in terms of *health and wholeness,* instead of just a part of your total self. Good regular medical care, proper exercise and diet, AND the prayer of faith for your health and wholeness go hand-in-hand, as we are demonstrating in Tulsa at the City of Faith Medical and Research Center on the Oral Roberts University campus.

At the City of Faith, physicians, nurses, prayer partners, and other health care professionals, all highly trained and skilled, work together as a Christ-centered team to help you into health and wholeness.

Third, work intellectually with God's system.

You have a mind, an intellect, which ties you together spiritually and physically. I know when I am functioning by my mind more than I am with my spirit or body, and vice versa.

Paul speaks of the "renewing of your mind" by the Holy Spirit" (Ephesians 4:23). So renew your mind through prayer, through studying God's Word, through hearing the Word of God preached and taught, and by educating your mind about God's world, its people, and the truths that have proven themselves through the ages. Also seek to learn new developing knowledge that is coming out of our space program. Read yourself full of good things (II Timothy 2:15).

Think. Think from the vantage point of your faith in God, knowing He is all-knowing. Think from the point of your humanness, dwelling on those most uplifting, creative and positive thoughts. Think only on good things (Philippians 4:8).

Study the Bible on how as a Christian indwelt by the Holy Spirit you can pray in tongues (your spirit by the power of the

Holy Spirit using your tongue through which to speak directly to God) the same way your mind uses your tongue to speak in your own language to God. Read about St. Paul's personal use of tongues, which is the "prayer and praise language of the Spirit" (I Corinthians 14:1,13,14). Learn to "interpret" what God says back to your mind AFTER you "pray in the Spirit" [tongues] (v. 13).

My own mind has blossomed, and continues to expand even beyond my own inborn ability, since I have developed in my personal devotion a regular habit daily of "praying with the Spirit and with my mind, also" (v. 15). I have proven this to myself so often that I wouldn't dare attempt anything without first going to prayer BOTH with my spirit AND with my mind, as St. Paul did (v. 14,15).

Study the Bible not only to learn better how to pray but also to interpret back what God is saying to you by His Holy Spirit.

Fourth, work financially with God's system.

A partner of mine said, "Oral, I have bad news. The stock market is down and I've lost most of my savings."

I said, "When did you as a Seed-Faith man, using God's Financial System, start making the stock market your source?"

He said, "Well, the stock market has been a pretty good place to invest over the years."

I said, "Sure, but if it is your financial source, it will let you down."

He said, "What are you trying to tell me?"

I said, "God is your Source. Everything else, and everybody else, is an instrument. Instruments are subject to man's manipulation. But God, your Source, who works through instruments, doesn't have to depend on any particular one. If your mind is on God as your Source, and one instrument doesn't work out, you still haven't lost, because God doesn't change or cease to be."

He said, "Well, just how will that work for me right now during my loss?"

I said, "Only one way. Plant a seed out of this loss."

He said, "Give something?"

I said, "Yes, give the seed for an equal benefit, one that will wipe out that loss and even give you a profit."

He said, "How do I do that?"

I said, "Go to the Word of God. Especially look at I Kings 17:8-24 where a widow woman had lost everything but her last meal. Out of her own need she gave the FIRST part of that meal to sustain the life of God's prophet, Elijah, for another day. It was her best seed."

He said, "What happened to her?"

I said, "Read it for yourself. Her loss was covered. Not only what she gave to the prophet was covered, but God increased her supply many times over. And God used that until it ended, then turned to another instrument for her supply. The same can happen to you as God opens the windows of heaven for you."

The miracle this man needed didn't happen in an instant. However, three months later he met me with a big smile. I said, "You look like something good has happened to you."

"It has," he replied.

"When did it happen?"

"I went immediately and planted an extra seed in God's work. It wasn't much, but it came out of my need and was the best of what I had left. Yesterday, three months later, my ship came in."

"What was in it?"

"Seven times more than I had lost financially, and best of all a spiritual blessing for my dry soul."

The scriptural way this partner worked with God's Financial System by his faith and seed of money, continues to have a powerful influence on his life. Today he sees money in the light of God's system and it has changed his entire outlook and expectancy to receive from God, his Source.

Money is the medium of exchange; that is, money or its equivalent. It represents your total being spiritually, mentally, financially — even emotionally. You can get sick financially, and you can get sick over your finances. I know. I've been there.

You are delicately tuned to money. Every person is, or he doesn't eat. You have to have money. God knows that. Even Jesus had to have money, and He always got it.

NO GIVING, NO LIVING

GIVING/LIVING is the most real and blessed thing you are going to experience on this earth. No giving, no living. Oh, you might exist. You might think you are making it. But to live, Christ said in John 10:10, is to "have life more abundantly." Life in FLOOD STAGE!

You start spiritually and mentally to put God first in your life, to make Him your Source, then go to work. As you work and earn, you give off the top, giving all your tithes and offerings because of WHO GOD IS . . . and who you are . . . planting it as a seed for God to "increase exceedingly," as He did for Abraham's faith-giving, which put him into GIVING/LIVING.

Speaking personally, the first thing Evelyn and I do with any money we earn is to give all our tithes and offerings first, then from that point start what I call our "sacrificial" giving. We know WHO GOD IS, and we know that our tithes and offerings belong to God. They are not ours. So we do not count it a sacrifice to give one-tenth, plus offerings, because that is already God's property. "The tithe is the Lord's" (Leviticus 27:30; Malachi 3:8). We also know who we are, and that as we worship and honor God by seeding our tithes and offerings to Him, we get the curse taken off our blessings which leads to FLOOD STAGE.

But for us there's a deeper stage of the Flood. To give a second tithe, a third, etc., has moved me — starting as a 17-year-old, just converted and healed — from a zero to the whole multiplication table! Yet I feel I have a long way to go in learning how to make my giving a seed of my faith so that I am a true Seed-Faith Christian . . . but I intend to get there.

MIX IN A "SPECIAL SEED"

Now I want to hold before you this thought. Learn to mix in a "special seed."

I remember on cool October mornings when I was a boy and we were picking our cotton, every now and then we would find a big watermelon growing between the rows. My brother Vaden and I would take our fists and smash it open and lift out the big juicy heart. My! I can still taste how good it was, and how it brightened our whole day as we gathered in our cotton crop.

You see, we learned to mix a handful of watermelon seed with a bushel of cotton seed and plant all of those seeds in the same field, but we had no trouble picking out which plant produced melons and which produced cotton. The soil produced both the cotton stalk and the watermelon vine. Planting a "special seed" gave us something beyond our harvest of cotton. We got a special uplift through the melons while we were picking our cotton crop.

You have financial needs. That means you have the opportunity to see for yourself that God's Blessing System really works in your finances. God will let you prove that His method works.

If you really want to see for yourself that God's method of blessing you really works in *your* finances, try mixing in a special seed over and above your regular "tithes and offerings" like I have illustrated here. But first start "giving tithes of all."

Then do something *extra* that will stand out in your field of blessing, the result of which will be as easy to pick out from all the other seed as it was for us to find the watermelon lying ripe and juicy between the cotton rows we were picking. Just as the soil produced both the cotton stalk and the watermelon vine, your tithe and the extra seed that you plant in the soil of the gospel will produce their own harvests from which you can expect to reap EXTRA — FLOOD STAGE!

Concerning this type of FLOOD STAGE reaping, focus your attention upon Galatians 6:7, "WHATSOEVER a man soweth, that shall he also REAP." Our God gives you His word that if you SOW it, He will GROW it — then you will REAP it.

This way of GIVING/LIVING is the heart of what I am teaching you from God's Word. GIVING/LIVING is part of me, because it is my faith in God. It is not a gimmick, but *a way of life* in Christ!

> What God has enabled me to build . . . the people I've reached . . . the souls saved, bodies healed, lives changed . . . the reality that I am somebody instead of a poor stuttering unsaved boy at the gates of death, causes the warm flood waters to wash over me to the point I think I will burst with gratitude, joy, and fulfillment.

Do I ever hurt financially? Oh, yes. At times the money stops and the bills pile up and when I look in the mirror I see myself as a man looking like if he died you would have to jack him up to bury him. But on the authority of the Word of God, which reminds me to go back to God's system (and I do), things start to change. That little trickle turns into a stream, then it widens into a river. Then FLOOD STAGE hits, and I am blessed and God can MAKE me a BLESSING to thousands of others. Then I try not to get back in the trickle stage.

The dawn is breaking and the sun is starting to burst through the clouds. A new day . . . A NEW DAY! . . . is starting. And I have only one more thing, including a prayer, to share with you, which is the best thing of all in this book. So don't miss this.

Before I pray, my thought is this:

What I am teaching is not magic. It's not going to happen automatically. Nor is it going to happen only because you have given your soul to Jesus and when you die you will go to heaven. It isn't even going to happen because God needs it. It's going to happen —

1. Because you have faith like Abraham had. Even if it's only the nature of Abraham's faith, but very small, you have it in Jesus Christ.

2. Because you believe God is Most High and that He has exalted Jesus' Name above everything that is named in this world and the world to come.

3. Because you believe in the principle of the seed — starting everything you do with a seed of your faith planted to God.

4. Because you believe your miracle harvests FOLLOW your seed sown, not the other way around.

5. Because you are stepping "now herewith" into giving tithes of all . . . into GIVING/LIVING . . . as your Seed-Faith and you will be regularly, rhythmically, joyously planting and receiving the rest of your life.

NOW I WANT YOU TO PRAY THIS PRAYER WITH ME:

Thank You, God, that You have the windows of heaven open to me. You are meeting my needs one by one, and at times Your blessings overflow me.

Thank You, God, that You are rebuking the devourer, the devil, from oppressing me with sickness. You are showing me ways to come into health and wholeness through Your natural

AND supernatural power, so that with better health I am helping others come into better health.

Thank You, God, for letting me prove You . . . and I *am* proving You with every seed I sow, by every miracle harvest I receive, and by every FLOOD STAGE harvest that I gather in. I am allowing it to overflow my life into other lives.

Thank You, God, that through the Name of Jesus and living in the rhythm of Seed-Faith, I am commanding the devil to take his hands off Your property — ME; and I am becoming freer and freer of what the devil can do to me and mine.

Thank You, God, that You change not, but I am changing. I do not expect something for nothing. I do not blame You for the bad things. I know You are a good God and I live in a state of constant expectancy of Your good things happening to me, then THROUGH me to many people.

Thank You, God, that because I know I am in Christ, my life is being made prosperous, healthy, and successful as an example of Your provability as the Most High God, Possessor of heaven and earth, Deliverer from all my enemies, and Multiplier of all my seed sown.

Thank You, God, that I trust You as my Source in good times and bad times, for I know You are making a way for me where there is no way in man's order of things.

Thank You, God, that You have honored me and given me the opportunity to worship You by "giving tithes of all" and "offerings." Not just once in a while. Not just when I feel like it. But I give as the "firstfruits" of everything, just as the farmer does in seedtime and harvest. Giving first, giving out of my need, giving my best seed every time. I make You my Source System because it will stand the test and prove You as my God. And beside You, there is no other. Amen and amen.

SUMMED UP

1. Without God, I cannot. Without me, He will not.
2. By my giving my tithes and offerings as seed to God, He is taking the curse off my blessings.
3. My windows which have been closed are now being opened. God is rebuking the devil from devouring me and pouring out blessings to move me into FLOOD STAGE.
4. I am to do the proving of God. No one else can do it for me. God is very provable.
5. I do not ask God to change His system to fit me, I will change to fit it.
6. I will work spiritually with God's system, then physically, intellectually, and financially.
7. I understand now that no giving/no living can be changed to GIVING/LIVING by me.
8. I will start by giving all my tithes and offerings as seed to God, then move into the deeper stages of the Flood by planting extra seeds so I can become a full Seed-Faith child of God.
9. I thank You, God, that You are my God, and beside You there is no other.

* * *

What does this chapter say to you? Write it down.

_____

_____

_____

_____

Don't Keep The Message In This Book To Yourself

Write today and request another copy of "Flood Stage" for you to give to a friend or loved one. I will send it to you free and postpaid for you to give to them personally.

Oral Roberts

Make It A Seed You Plant In Their Life!

YES, I WANT TO BE MADE A BLESSING TO SOMEONE TODAY!

☐ Oral Roberts, God has blessed me through reading this book. Now I want to plant a seed and be made a blessing to someone else by giving them their own personal copy of FLOOD STAGE. Please rush another FREE copy to me so I can help the person I have on my heart receive the miracles they need.

MY NAME _____

ADDRESS _____ 176

CITY _____ STATE_____ ZIP_____

Mail coupon to: Oral Roberts, Tulsa, Oklahoma 74171

170   **In Canada: Oral Roberts, Toronto, Ontario M4P2G2**

Miracle of SEED-FAITH...

A book that's changed the lives of millions!

If you would like to know more about the Seed-Faith way of life — the GIVING/LIVING I've talked so much about in the FLOOD STAGE book — I highly recommend that you write me today for a copy of MIRACLE OF SEED-FAITH.

When I wrote MIRACLE OF SEED-FAITH in 1970, it was a revolutionary concept on giving to God and receiving back from Him. Since that time, it has been read by over 3 1/2 million families...families whose lives have been changed!

Write me today for your free personal copy.

☐ Yes, I want to know more about the Seed-Faith way of life. Please send me my free personal copy of MIRACLE OF SEED-FAITH.

MY NAME _____

175

ADDRESS _____

CITY _____ STATE_____ ZIP_____

171

Mail coupon to: Oral Roberts, Tulsa, Oklahoma 74171
In Canada: Oral Roberts, Toronto, Ontario M4P2G2

Prayer Tower, Oral Roberts University campus

When you're troubled and needing prayer, don't try to handle it alone. Call the Prayer Tower, where. . .

You Have a Partner in Prayer

The Abundant Life Prayer Group receives almost 2,000 phone calls a day for prayer. Seven days a week, 24 hours a day, a caring prayer partner will take your call and agree with you in prayer for the miracle you need.

Dial 918 ● 492-7777

I CARE ABOUT YOU

   I want to invite you to write me. When you tell me what you're going through, I can know better how to write you back. . .and how to pray and help you believe God for the miracles you need. I care about you. I want to encourage you in the Lord and help you learn to get your needs met. Simply address your letter to:

Oral Roberts
Tulsa, Oklahoma 74171
In Canada write:
Oral Roberts
Toronto, Ontario M4P2G2

Notes

Notes